AMERICAN IMPERIALISM
Viewpoints of United States
Foreign Policy, 1898-1941

Reproduced with the cooperation of the
Hoover Institution of War, Revolution and Peace,
Stanford University, Stanford, California

CHANGING
THE COLONIAL CLIMATE

Rexford Guy Tugwell

ARNO PRESS & THE NEW YORK TIMES
New York ★ 1970

Collection Created and Selected
by
CHARLES GREGG OF GREGG PRESS

Reprinted from a copy in The Hoover Institution Library

Library of Congress Catalog Card Number: 70-111734
ISBN 0-405-02052-X

ISBN for complete set: 0-405-02000-7

[1942?]

Reprint Edition 1970 by Arno Press Inc.
Manufactured in the United States of America

CHANGING
THE
COLONIAL
CLIMATE

THE STORY, FROM HIS
OFFICIAL MESSAGES, OF
GOVERNOR REXFORD GUY
TUGWELL'S EFFORTS TO
BRING DEMOCRACY TO AN
ISLAND POSSESSION WHICH
SERVES THE UNITED NATIONS
AS A WARBASE.

Few have paused to note that after Tugwell moves on from a troubled intellectual frontier, clearings have a way of appearing amongst the political trees and in those clearings rise the outposts of future United States policy.

—Wide World News.

The Carribbean island of Puerto Rico has been under political subjection ever since Christopher Columbus discovered it in 1493. It was a colony of Spain until 1898, when the United States became sovereign. Its people have been struggling for freedom for more than a hundred years. They hope and expect that out of the peace settlement after this war there will come for them greater freedom, a more dignified status. They believe that the Atlantic Charter has for them a special meaning. After forty years, the promise of General Miles seems to them about to be redeemed.

If they are to make progress in their ambition, the Puerto Ricans must maintain the confidence and respect of the people of the United States. And the people of the United States, for the sake of their national safety, must have the friendship of this island which serves us as a war base.

So that faith may be kept on both sides, it is necessary for the role of the island's Governor, Rexford Guy Tugwell, holder of the dual responsibility of being President Roosevelt's representative and administrative head of the Puerto Rican government, to be understood. Here, in the Governor's own words, is the story of what he is and what he has tried to do.

Out of a man's utterances, it is possible to choose a few representative statements which mark the channel of his thought.

That is what has been done in the following collection of messages from Governor Tugwell to the Puerto Rican people. The selection and explanatory comments are made by John Lear, Coordinator of Information for Puerto Rico.

Being Governor of Puerto Rico is unquestionably one of the most difficult administrative tasks in the world. The colonial status of the island is reflected in its devious politics. Appointment by the President frees the Governor from dependence on any of the constantly shifting parties, yet leaves him prey to attack by any party which is dissatisfied. No Governor ever has escaped this, but those who believed most in laissez-faire government suffered least. Since the United States took Puerto Rico from Spain in 1898, laissez-faire has meant acceptance of political, economic and social domination by a small private oligarchy.

To understand this is to understand how Governor Tugwell can be the most popular executive in the history of the island, can command a working majority in support of his program in the four legislative sessions of his first year in office, and yet can be made to appear on the mainland as a hated tyrant.

Mr. Tugwell became Governor in September of 1942. But the story of his fight against the feudalism of sugar began long before that. It was in 1934, while he was Assistant United States Secretary of Agriculture, that he joined, quite accidentally, the battle of Puerto Ricans to free themselves from absentee landlords. He came to the island to plan expansion of the only tropical rain forest under the American flag, and to establish a C. C. C. unit to put jobless young men back to work on the land. He stayed, briefly, to discuss how marginal acreage could be turned from sugar to other crops and thus diversify the base of the island's economy. Out of his visit came a land distribution and resettlement scheme known as the Chardon Plan, named for one of the men who wrote it, Dr. Carlos E. Chardon. And out of the Chardon Plan came the PRRA, which began the work of reconstruction only to lose support in Congress and reduce its effectiveness for want of funds.

The PRRA (Puerto Rico Reconstruction Administration) was set up as a Federal agency. As such, it was attacked as a "*super-government.*" *PRRA, its insular opponents said, should be made part of the insular administration. The real reason for opposition was that it could not be controlled. The ostensible reason is especially interesting because the same group, out of power today, is attacking Governor Tugwell's insular administration as a "super-government" and is asking Federal control of the insular government through establishment of an inter-departmental administrator to be sent from Washington. The insincerity of both positions is quite obvious. What is wanted is the disposition of the patronage involved. Any arrangement useful for this purpose would be acceptable.*

The PRRA began its work with eager anticipation among Puerto Ricans that their economic difficulty might at last be solved. And they, themselves, taking new heart, began the enforcement of the 500 acre limitation which in 1901 the Congress had written into the Organic Act.

The sugar corporations carried the fight up to the United States Supreme Court, and finally lost. Whereupon the Puerto Rican legislature took new courage and passed a land law of its own to enforce the 500 acre limitation.

All this had a natural effect on politics. Poor people who had sold their votes for years because they saw no way to beat the system were open to argument. In 1940 the argument came. Luis Muñoz Marín, whose father had won the equivalent of modern statehood for Puerto Rico in nineteenth century Spain and later pushed the island's present territorial constitution through Congress, campaigned for "Bread! Land! Liberty!" His Popular Party won. He became President of the Senate.

That was in November. In December, Mr. Tugwell came again into direct participation in the affairs of the island, this time as a representative of Secretary of Interior Ickes, charged with making a report.

INVESTIGATION INTO ADMINISTRATIVE RESPONSIBILITIES UNDER THE FIVE HUNDRED ACRE LIMITATION ON LAND HOLDINGS IN THE ORGANIC ACT FOR PUERTO RICO

THE HONORABLE,
THE SECRETARY OF THE INTERIOR;

SIR:

I

You will remember, I think, that when you telephoned me on December 24, 1940 with a request that I undertake an investigation of responsibilities for enforcement of the so-called Five Hundred Acre Provision in the Organic Act which is the basic law of Puerto Rico, you found me curious but entirely uninformed. I think it is true to say also that you yourself were a little undecided as to whether the limitation imposed in the Act had been a wise one and whether it could be made to serve a useful purpose in bettering conditions in Puerto Rico.

Preliminary investigation revealed that the question was an administrative one; the limitation existed even if it had been lengthily ignored; but also it was one which involved some judgment as to the conditions under which alienation should take place and what sort of pattern should be substituted for the old one. You asked for suggestions as to procedure. My first one was that a Commission be appointed to investigate; it should include several experts in government and planning as well as in agricultural techniques. I sent you a list of suggestions for membership on the same day you called. This proved to be impractical since Congress has severely limited the investigating powers of the executive departments. Also there seemed to be no funds with which experts could be paid. The weeks which followed our first conversation were spent in exploration of procedure for the investigation itself. They resulted in a continuous growth of interest in the problem but also in a gradual reduction in the equipment which could be expected to be made available. Finally, I was appointed as Special Assistant to the Secretary, after getting the necessary approval from Mayor La-Guardia. As to other members of a commission or committe, the most that could be expected was that their services would

11

be "requested" from other Departments. As it turned out, no Department but Agriculture seemed necessarily involved and the officials of that Department made no difficulty about supplying the services (together with expenses) of the several experts who collaborated. All of them contributed to the work with readiness and ability.

These preliminaries, although somewhat prolonged and annoying, were finally got over, and by January 28 a group was made up consisting, after several substitutions, of: Mr. George S. Mitchell, Assistant Administrator of the Farm Security Administration; Mr. Ivy Duggan, Director of the Southern Division of the Agricultural Adjustment Administration; Mr. Russell Lord, Counselor of the Commodity Credit Corporation; Mr. Carl Robbins, President of the Commodity Credit Corporation; Mr. Rafael Menéndez Ramos, Dean of the College of Agriculture and Mechanic Arts, Mayagüez, P. R.; Mr. Monroe Oppenheimer, of the Solicitor's Office of the U. S. Department of Agriculture in charge of the legal work of the Farm Security Administration; Mr. Benjamin V. Cohen, General Counsel of the Power Policy Committee; Mr. Henry A. Hirshberg, General Counsel for the Puerto Rico Reconstruction Administration; Mr. Rupert Emerson, Director of the Division of Territories and Island Possessions; Mr. Leon H. Cubberley, Executive Secretary, and Mrs. Grace Tugwell, Assistant.

A temporary office was set up in the Department of the Interior and such background material as could be gathered was circulated. There were still some difficult relations which had to be resolved by negotiation. The Office of Territories and Island Possessions was involved, but Mr. Rupert Emerson, who was then its Director, proved to be helpful and indeed became a valuable member of the original group. Correspondence with the Governor's Office and the Attorney General's Office in Puerto Rico [1] and with various insular agricultural specialists resulted in the addition of Mr. Menéndez Ramos to the group and the establishment of workable relations with insular officials conducting cases and carrying on administration.

Material available for study at that time included the Report of the Puerto Rico Policy Commission (Chardon

[1] At that time Mr. Guy J. Swope was Governor and Mr. George A. Malcolm was Attorney General.

Plan) of 1934; the Zimmerman Report of 1938; the Brookings Institute Survey of 1930, *Porto Rico and Its Problems;* briefs, orders, memoranda, and decisions in the Rubert Hermanos and Fajardo cases; various examinations of economic conditions and certain health surveys, particularly those of Dr. Pérez; reports having to do with the experience in in alienating the so-called Friar Lands in the Philippines; reports of Governors and Bureau heads and of the Puerto Rico Reconstruction Administration; the Joint Resolution of Congress of 1900; the Corporation Law of Puerto Rico; and various Congressional hearings looking toward revision of the Joint Resolution.

So far as I myself was concerned, the study of these materials and conferences with various responsible officials recalled to my mind problems with which I had been familiar a few years ago and revived certain issues with which I had dealt as an official and now discovered to be still unsettled. The first mentioned of these materials, the Chardon Plan, which had led to setting up the Puerto Rico Reconstruction Administration, had been a study which I, as Assistant Secretary of Agriculture, had requested to be made and which I had had at least some part in implementing by my insistence, as an official, that benefit payments going to sugar producers under the first Agricultural Adjustment Act of 1933, should be reserved "for the benefit of agriculture in Puerto Rico" rather than benefit payments to particular individuals and corporations. Others of those whose advice I expected to draw on had been more or less directly concerned with the sugar industry, which was obviously more affected than any other by the five-hundred-acre limitation, or as officials responsible for the administration of various related laws. Mr. Robbins had been a member of the Sugar Section of the Agricultural Adjustment Administration and was now President of the Commodity Credit Corporation; Mr. Duggan was Director of the Southern Division of the Agricultural Adjustment Admin-

---

(1) This policy did not survive long. The sugar lobbyists had first assumed the attitude of opposing everything and could not, therefore, object to the method proposed for the use of benefit payments. As soon as they retreated from the first position, they were able to secure benefit payments for their principals. These benefits have been attached to the land ever since. They are, of course, the source of the most rabid opposition to the disposal of the large estates.

Over $11,000,000 was collected between 1 July 1933, and 10 April 1936, as processing taxes on Puerto Rican sugar. Of this, about $2,300,000 was expended directly from the Trust Fund and the balance was transferred to Emergency Relief. Of this amount, some at least went to finance soil surveys, agricultural research, rural rehabilitation, etc.—mostly projects later taken over and carried on by P.R.R.A., which was financed from Relief funds.

13

istration; Mr. Menéndez Ramos was one of the authors of the Chardon Plan and, of course, Dean of the College of Agriculture and Mechanic Arts of the University of Puerto Rico; Mr. Oppenheimer had been General Counsel of the Farm Security Administration and was now Chief, Farm Security Division, Office of the Solicitor, U. S. Department of Agriculture; Mr. Hirshberg was General Counsel for the Puerto Rico Reconstruction Administration; Mr. George S. Mitchell was Assistant Administrator of the Farm Security Administration.

II

There have been several theories as to how Congress came to put into the Joint Resolution of 1900 the prohibition against a corporation engaged in agriculture in Puerto Rico owning more than five hundred acres of land. One was that it was the result of anti-American machinations on the part of large Spanish landowners. This theory, when we came to studying it, however, left to be explained how, when the United States had just defeated Spain in war and had taken over from her the insular colony, the American Congress should have been in any way tender of the feelings of Spanish landowners. And certainly it was difficult to understand how this might explain a prohibition against American corporations which did not extend to the Spanish operating as individuals. The crux of this contention was, of course, that the United States, being a more advanced country in the technique of industrial organization, could have been expected to enter Puerto Rican industry, which was largerly agricultural, only with corporate enterprises. The Spanish capitalist, being an individualist, would not adopt the corporate form. Therefore, the United States Congress, being unsophisticated in such matters and having just been through several decades in which prejudice against corporations was very strong, was fooled into using its prejudices blindly in such a way as to injure Americans and to favor the Spanish. There is, so far as I have been able to discover, little to support such an argument. The only evidence is a suspicion voiced by Senator Tillman when the five hundred-acre limitation was inserted by the House and Senate conferees; and this suspicion was argued away by the author of the bill.[1] There is, however, no real refutation of it; and there is no doubt that, whether intended or not, some such result has come about.

It will, of course, be recalled that this was the age of trust-busting and that the limitation on Puerto Rican corporations was not the only action in which Congress expressed a prejudice against big business in general and the corporate form of it in particular.

A more tenable theory, perhaps, than the one which suggests the machinations of Spanish landlords, rests merely on the well-known prejudices of legislators at the turn of the century. It is certainly not inconsistent with other items of history to infer that it was a simple reaction to the word "corporation" and that what was intended was really the protection of small and middle-size farmers—as they have since been protected elsewhere, and were at that time also in the process of being protected in the Philippines—from competition with corporations. It may have been part of the agrarianism of the time, of the current prejudice in favor of the small farmer and businessman and against developments in industry which they seemed unable to resist except by resort to restrictive legislation.

Another theory which, on the face of it, would seem more tenable than that of a diplomatic victory of the Spanish landlords, and not so naive as mere dislike of corporations, is that which attributes the prohibition to the lobbyists and legislators from other areas of sugar production. The legislative record of the Joint Resolution alone reveals little of the purposes, but the legislative record of the Organic Act (which the Joint Resolution amended and which passed only 12 days

---

(1) "I notice a limitation in the report upon the amount of land any corporation shall be allowed to own. We put a similar provision in the Hawaiian bill the other day, and it occurred to me that the purpose of it was to give the present corporations in Hawaii—I do not know whether they are any in Porto Rico or not—but I thought the purpose of the Hawaiian legislation was to give a monopoly to existing sugar mills and corporations growing sugar cane; and if the purpose of this bill is to limit the erection of new cane mills and sugar-making machinery to existing corporations, so as to create an additional monopoly under the guise of preventing monopolies, then I should object very strenuously to this or any other similar measure . . ." Mr. Tillman. p. 4852, *Congressional Record*, 30 April 1900.
"That is one of the provisions that was adopted in the conference against my objection. The House of Representatives had inserted a provision that no corporation should be allowed to engage in agriculture. That was objected to on the part of the Senate conferees. It was thought that the coffee plantations and sugar plantations and tobacco plantations were in such a condition that they needed capital beyond anything else possible, and that if any corporation wanted to engage in that business we could afford to leave the regulation of the terms and conditions upon which they should so engage to the local authorities who are given full legislative power. Finally, as a result of it all, and for the purpose of compromising differences . . . . . it was proposed on the part of the House conferees that that section might go out if we would insert what has been reported . . . . . the idea being to prevent a monopolizing on the part of anybody of the lands in Porto Rico." Mr. Foraker, p. 4852, *Congressional Record*, 30 April 1900.

15

prior to the Joint Resolution) read in conjunction with the history of the Joint Resolution, reveals some support for this theory.

The original H. R. 8245, which was to become the Organic Act of Puerto Rico, was introduced on 19 January 1900 by the Republican majority-leader in the House upon instructions contained in a message from the President to provide temporary revenue for the new possession. The President had asked for free trade in his message [1] and the bill as originally introduced was a free trade bill. Soon thereafter, however, the Committee amended the bill to provide for the imposition of a tariff amounting to 25 per cent of the Dingley Tariff (the regular tariff schedule then in effect on trade between the United States and foreign countries) on trade between the United States and Puerto Rico, the funds so collected to be placed at the disposal of the President to be used for the benefit of Puerto Rico.[2] The Republicans claimed that their about-face was not at variance with the President's instructions since the funds collected under the tariff would be returned to Puerto Rico.[3] But there was apparently a storm of protest against this amendment to the bill. The implication was that pressure from mainland and Hawaiian sugar interests had induced the Republican Party to depart from the President's free trade instructions. The Democrats

---

(1) "Our plain duty is to abolish all customs tariffs between the United States and Puerto Rico, and give her products free access to our markets." President's message to Congress, December 1899 as quoted p. 2423, *Congressional Record* — House, 28 February 1900.

(2) Section 3 of H. R. 8245 "That after the passage of this act all merchandise coming into the United States from Puerto Rico and coming into Puerto Rico from the United States shall be entered at the several ports of entry upon payment of 25 per cent of the duties which are required to be levied, collected, and paid upon like articles of merchandise imported from foreign countries . . . . ."

Section 4 "That the customs duties collected in Puerto Rico in pursuance of this act, less the cost of collecting the same, and the gross amount of all collections of customs in the United States upon articles of merchandise coming from Puerto Rico shall not be covered into the general fund of the Treasury, but shall be held as a separate fund, and shall be placed at the disposal of the President to be used for the government and benefit of Puerto Rico until otherwise provided by law." P. 2401, *Congressional Record—House,* 28 February 1900.

(3) "The President of the United States in his annual message recommended that the Congress should abolish all customs tariffs between Puerto Rico and the United States, and should admit their products to our markets without duty . . . . It was evidently the purpose of the President, and the only purpose which he had, to do something to give that people a chance to rebuild its fallen fortunes and to begin anew its commercial and industrial life. Now, notwithstanding the abuse that has been heaped upon this bill on this floor and in the public press, I undertake to say that it does in substance exactly what the President had in mind to do . . . Under this bill . . . the entire fund—all collected here and all collected there—being expressly devoted to public uses in connection with their local government. In that view of the case the injustice will appear which has been done to the Ways and Means Committee by gentlemen on our own side of the House, by our friends on the other side, and by an organized coercion of public opinion elsewhere in the United States . . . . ." Mr. Dolliver, (Republican). *Congressional Record—House, p. 2342, 27 February 1900.

16

charged openly that the sugar trust had bribed the Republican Administration by promising financial support in the coming campaign.[1]

The Republicans replied that the sugar trusts were asking for free trade and were opposed to the bill. They submitted, in support of their case, a statement from the American Sugar Refining Company[2] to that effect, as well as the fact that a suit had been brought against the Federal Government by this same Company to recover tariffs already paid on raw sugar importations (the full Dingley tariff was in effect until the passage of the bill).[3]

What it was doubtless hoped would be overlooked was the fact that the American Sugar Refining Company was engaged in *refining* sugar, not in producing it, and was indeed interested in cheap raw sugar. It is significant that the mainland and Hawaiian producers made no such statement for quotation by the Republicans to support their innocence. There was not one sugar trust, but several.

It is true that the Democrats were not altogether altruistic in their fight against the bill. They must have been reached by the pressure of the refiners because they attempted to cover the tariffs referred to above by offering an amendment which would have returned them "to the persons from whom

---

[1] "But, Mr. Chairman, not only did the President lay down what our 'plain duty' was in inviting Congress to at once establish free trade with Puerto Rico, but the chairman of the Ways and Means Committee, the chosen leader of the Republican majority on this floor, promptly introduced a bill to enable the President to fulfill his 'plain duty' and thus provide 'free trade' with Puerto Rico."

"But a sudden change came over the President and his Republican majority in this House that no one seems able to account for. Certainly a change which no one . . . has dared to explain."

"Perhaps the specter of the heavy hand of an unfriendly trust loomed up with one hand closing the door of a great safe and the finger of the other hand pointing to an approaching storm, on the clouds of which could be seen the words, Campaign of 1900 . . ." Mr. Otey, *Congressional Record*—House, 28 February 1900, p. 2409.

"Mr. Speaker, a gentleman of this city, a reputable local writer on one of our papers here, the Evening Staff, told him that a Representative on your side, a Republican, told him that this bill would pass because a large contribution had been promised by the trusts of this country to your campaign fund. Now, you do not investigate the matter. The name of the writer of that statement is known . . . The name of the writer is John P. Miller . . ." Mr. Richardson, (Dem.), p. 4030, *Congressional Record*—House, 11 April 1900.

[2] "New York, March 29 (1900)—"President Havemeyer of the American Sugar Refining Company, . . . in discussing the whole situation, was plain and outspoken regarding the position of Porto Rico and the Philippines, and declared that there was no reason in the world why sugars should not be admitted free of duty from these countries." Quoted by Mr. Watson, Republican, p. 4032, *Congressional Record*—House, 11 April 1900.

[3] "It will be remembered that the full Dingley tariff is yet in operation between this country and Porto Rico, and that under its operation $1,800,000 was collected as duty on sugar . . . coming into this country from Porto Rico between the date of the acquisition of that island and the 1st day of January, 1900. The American sugar trust and those representing its interests claim now that they paid that duty . . . and are seeking to recover it back from the Government . . . Do we suppose for a moment that this great sugar trust is in court in New York seeking to recover back the tariff duty which it alleges it has paid, and at the same time is here seeking to have a tariff duty imposed upon itself and its own products? . . ." Mr. Watson, (Republican), p. 4035, *Congressional Record*—House, 11 April 1900.

they were collected''[1] and they also offered a resolution to admit raw sugar free of duty.[2]

Although the Republicans claimed that sugar production in Puerto Rico offered little competition,[3] there seems to be little doubt that pressure from mainland and Hawaiian sugar *producers* was brought to bear on the Administration. Of pressure from the Hawaiian interests there is little evidence other than accusations from the other side of the House:[4] But the American Beet Sugar Association (which already represented thirty beet sugar factories in 12 different states) in its own testimony before the House Committee on Insular Affairs admitted that it was not so much afraid of present competition from Puerto Rican sugar as that *large investments would go into Puerto Rico,* if restrictions were not imposed, and in that way offer real competition.[5] Indeed, the author of the Senate version of this bill, Senator Foraker, admitted on the floor of the Senate that he looked toward *future protection.*[6] These statements supply the key to the five hundred acre prohibition. For the criticism was so sharp and prolonged (indeed several Republicans bolted and refused their support[7]) that the Administration was forced to

(1) P. 4069, *Congressional Record*—House, 11 April 1900.

(2) ''. . . Resolved by the Senate and House of Representatives of the United States of America in Congress assembled, That from and after the passage of this resolution all kinds of sugar, molasses, and everything entering into the manufacture of sugars shall be admitted free of duty from Porto Rico and Cuba.'' P. 4069, *Congressional Record*—House, 11 April 1900.

(3) ''I know that it is true that Senator Foraker, in his report upon the bill for the temporary government for Puerto Rico, and Mr. Payne, in his report upon this bill, both take the position that the production of sugar and tobacco in the island is so insignfiicant compared with the production and consumption in the United States that it could not affect the prices of these commodities to the consumer, and that therefore they would not enter into competition with the home production . . .'' Mr. Bromwell, *Congressional Record*—House, 21 February 1900.

(4) ''Behold the iniquity of this bill on sugar. Everybody knows that the sugar made in the Hawaiian Islands, amounting to 300,000 tons, shall come in free. Why that? Because Claud Spreckles, a Republican potential in the councils of the Republican party, owns the entire sugar industry of Hawaii. In Hawaii sugar is raised by a system of contract labor amounting to slavery; and yet we give to his 300,000 tons of sugar a free American market, and while on this 60,000 tons of Puerto Rico sugar we impose a duty under this bill . . .'' Mr. Swanson, Dem., *Congressional Record*—House, 28 February 1900, p. 2415.

''I believe that those great monopolies which have grown up under the fostering care of a high protective tariff are solely responsible for the sudden change of front of the Republican Party upon this great question . . .'' Mr. Jones, Dem., *Congressional Record*—House, p. 2427, 28 February 1900.

(5) ''What we claim is this: While we are perfectly willing to let them come in, we think they would largely increase their production of sugar . . . and we claim they are taking and will take in time a larger proportion of our market from us, and we would like to have some tariff put up against them . . . what I claim is large investments will go into Puerto Rico in the sugar business as soon as it is found that this immense profit can be made.'' *Congressional Record*—House, p. 2272, 26 February 1900.

(6) ''I do not think that there is any better philanthropy than that which seeks to protect the wage-worker and the capital of this country from unjust competition from abroad. We fear no competition from Puerto Rico; that has nothing to do with it; but in the contingency I have pointed out there may and would come a competition which would be prejudicial; and if we are wise, we will now legislate to prepare the way for protection when that trouble comes.'' P. 2651, *Congressional Record*—Senate, 8 March 1900.

(7) ''As a Republican I have always been an ardent defender of the principles of that great Party . . . I am of the profound conviction that the measure is wrong in principle . . .'' Mr. Crumpacker, *Congressional Record*—House, p. 4045, 11 April 1900.

retreat from its position even before the bill left the House. The tariff provision was reduced from 25 per cent of the Dingley Tariff to 15 per cent and, even more significant, its enforcement was limited to two years.[1] This left continental interests with only temporary protection against Puerto Rican sugar competition.

Apparently, the Senate conferees had already decided to accept the situation, because one hour after the bill was received from the House and referred to the Senate Committee on Pacific Islands and Puerto Rico it was reported out by the Chairman of that Committee, Senator Foraker, with all but the title of the House version deleted and the Senate measure substituted. This provided for a permanent civil government in Puerto Rico but retained the 15 per cent tariff with its two-year limitation.

The measure was passed in this form on 12 April 1900. It obviously left something else to be done.

The Joint Resolution (S. R. 116) was introduced on 18 April 1900 (six days after the passage of the Organic Act) by the Chairman of the Committee on Pacific Islands and Porto Rico, Senator Foraker (the author of the Organic Act), to implement a recommendation from the President for the continuation of the existing military government pending the setting up of the permanent civil government provided for under the Organic Act.[2] The Joint Resolution introduced by Senator Foraker provided for no more than the message asked except that it limited the duration of the extension to

---

(1) "The fact that this bill limits the duration of the proposed tariff is an admission by its framers that in principle and practice it is wrong. The action of the Senate, acquiesced in by the Committee on Ways and Means of this House, in making the tariff merely nominal, to remain in force only a short time, is an admission that it is unjustifiable . . ." Mr. Warner, Democrat, *Congressional Record*—House, 11 April 1900.

(2) *Congressional Record*—Senate, p. 4370, 18 April 1900. To the Senate and House of Representatives:

The time remaining before the 1st day of May, when the act of April 12, 1900, entitled "An act temporarily to provide revenues and a civil government for Porto Rico, and for other purposes," will take effect, appears to be insufficient for the careful inquiry and consideration requisite to the proper selection of suitable persons to fill the important civil offices provided for by the act. The powers of the present government will cease when the act takes effect, and some new authority will be necessary to enable the officers now performing the various duties of civil government in the island to continue the performance of those duties until the officers who are to perform similar duties under the new government shall have been appointed and qualified. That authority can not well be given at present by temporary appointments of the existing officers to positions under the act, for the reason that many of the existing officers are officers of the Army detailed to the performance of civil duties, and section 1222 of the Revised Statutes would prevent them from accepting such temporary appointments under the penalty of losing their commissions. The selection of the new officers and the organization of the new government under the act referred to will be accomplished with all practicable speed, but in order that it may be properly accomplished, I recommend the passage of a joint resolution to obviate the difficulty above stated.

WILLIAM McKINLEY.

Executive Mansion, April 18, 1900.

19

1 August 1900.[1]   It passed the Senate in that form with little debate on 19 April 1900.   When the Joint Resolution arrived in the House it was referred to the Committee on Insular Affairs, the committee which had heard the appeal of the beet sugar interests for tariff restrictions in the Organic Act. And it was when that body reported the Joint Resolution for consideration by the House that the restriction against corporate agricultural enterprise first appeared.   This first one was not a very forceful restriction—it provided no specific limitation beyond such as might "be reasonably necessary to carry out the purposes for which it was created".[2]   The amendment seems to have been favored also by the minority in the House Committee which gave as its reasons for introducing the amendment a desire to protect the population of Puerto Rico against exploitation by "the great corporations of this country"[3]   There was some objection that the success of the sugar industry depended upon "the aggregation of capital by corporations and by central mills"[4] but the Committee's opinion "that it would not be for the interest of a million people, crowded upon a territory 100 by 40 miles in extent, to have one corporation own all, or substantially all,

---

[1] *Congressional Record*—Senate, p. 4371, 18 April 1900.

"Resolved, etc.   That until the officers to fill any office provided for by the act of April 12, 1900, entitled 'An act temporarily to provide revenues and a civil government for Porto Rico, and for other purposes,' shall have been appointed and qualified, the officer or officers now performing the civil duties pertaining to such office may continue to perform the same under the authority of said act; and no officer of the Army shall lose his commission by reason thereof; *Provided*, That nothing herein contained shall be held to extend the time for the appointment and qualification of any such officers beyond the 1st day of August 1900."

[2] "No corporation shall be authorized to conduct the business of buying and selling real estate, of issuing currency, or of engaging in agriculture, or permitted to hold or own real estate, except such as may be reasonably necessary to enable it to carry out the purposes for which it was created. Banking corporations, however, may be authorized to loan funds upon real estate security, and to purchase real estate when necessary for the collection of loans, but they shall dispose of all real estate so obtained within five years after receiving the title.   Corporations other than those organized in Porto Rico, and doing business therein, shall be bound by the provisions of this section so far as they are applicable." *Congressional Record*—House, p. 4613, 24 April 1900.

[3] "Mr. Speaker, speaking for the minority members of the Committee on Insular Affairs, I wish to express a hope that this joint resolution, as amended by that committee, may be passed . . . The third section of the joint resolution, or second amendment . . . provides that no corporation shall be chartered in Porto Rico for the purpose of carrying on the business of agriculture, and that no corporation shall be chartered for the purpose of engaging in the buying and selling of real estate.   It is well known to the members of this House that the Island of Porto Rico is only about 95 miles long and about 35 or 40 miles wide.   It is well known also that it contains a denser population than any other country on the globe and that only a small part of the soil of the island is adapted to the cultivation of sugar cane.   Unless these amendments are adopted I believe that it is almost certain that within the shortest period possible after the government provided for by the act of April 12 has been organized and put into operation the *great corporations of this country will own every single acre of the sugar and tobacco lands of this most fertile island*. And if that shall become the case, then the condition of the population will, I believe, be reduced to one of absolute servitude.   The people of Porto Rico will be driven to cultivate these lands for those corporations at whatever daily wage they choose to pay them . . ." Mr. Jones, *Congressional Record*—House, 24 April 1900, p. 4619.

[4] Mr. Hill (Conn. Dem.), p. 4620, *Congressional Record*—House, 24 April 1900.

20

the land''[1] seems to have been accepted, for the amendments were adopted by the House and referred back to the Senate. On 24 April 1900 Senator Foraker moved to disagree to the amendments of the House and requested that conferees be appointed.[2] On 25 April 1900, Mr. Cooper (the Republican Manager) moved that the House insist on its amendments and House conferees were appointed.[3] On 30 April 1900 the report of the joint conference was submitted to the Senate. The specific limitation of five hundred acres had been introduced in conference. That this was an ''addition of legislative matters'' and therefore an extraordinary proceeding is perhaps academic to recall at this late date.[4] Senator Foraker explained what had gone on in conference as follows:

''If the Senator will allow me a moment, I will explain to him how that came about. The House of Representatives had inserted a provision that no corporation should be allowed to engage in agriculture. That was objected to on the part of the Senate conferees. It was thought that the coffee plantations and sugar plantations and tobacco plantations were in such a condition that they needed capital beyond anything else possibly, and that if any corporation wanted to engage in that business we could afford to leave the regulation of the terms and conditions upon which they should so engage to the local authorities, who are given full legislative power.

''Finally, as the result of it all, and for the purpose of compromising the differences which seemed difficult to overcome, it was proposed on the part of the House conferees that that section might go out if we would insert what has been reported, namely: That corporations hereafter organized for the purpose of engaging in agriculture should be restricted by their charters to the ownership of not more than 500 acres of land, and that no man connected in any capacity with a corporation engaged in agriculture should be allowed to be interest in any other corporation that was engaged in agriculture, the idea being to prevent a monopolizing on the part of anybody of the lands in Porto Rico.''[5]

The Committee of Conference had delayed submitting the Joint Resolution until the day before the deadline, 30 April 1900. The Organic Act was to become effective on 1 May and

(1) ''People there can not cross imaginary State lines and go into other states as they can here in crowded and populous communities . . . They can not go anywhere. They are obliged to stay in the island of Porto Rico, and the ownership of the land has a special significance in that limited and crowded space. Therefore, this legislation must not be taken as establishing a precedent for legislation anywhere else. We establish this legislation for Porto Rico because of the conditions that obtain in that crowded island . . .'' Mr. Cooper, (Wis., Rep.) p. 4621, 24 April 1900, Congressional Record—House.
(2) P. 4586, Congressional Record—Senate.
(3) P. 4686, Congressional Record—House.
(4) ''That the Senate recede from its disagreement to the amendment of the House section 3, and agree to the same amended as follows: . . . by inserting after the word 'created' the following: 'and every corporation hereafter authorized to engage in agriculture shall by its charter be restricted to the ownership and control of not to exceed 500 acres of land; and this provision shall be held to prevent any member of a corporation engaged in agriculture from being in any wise interested in any other corporation engaged in agriculture'.'' Conference report on S. R. 116, 30 April 1900, p. 4850, Congressional Record—Senate.
(5) Sen. Foraker, p. 4852, Congressional Record—Senate, 30 April, 1900. See also note, p. 4.

Puerto Rico would be without governing officials unless the first section of the Joint Resolution were passed providing for the extension of the existing military government. It was on the basis of this argument that the Chairman of the Committee on Pacific Islands and Puerto Rico, Senator Foraker, asked, and got, agreement from the Senate on the Joint Resolution with no more than a verbal reading.[1] Little notice was taken of the five hundred acre restriction. Only one member of the Senate questioned it, and he thought that it might have been added to protect existing monopolies on the island.[2] On being assured by the Chairman of the Committee that its purpose was "to prevent monopolies now in existence from keeping out competitors"[3] he withdrew his objection. The Joint Resolution as presented by the Committee was agreed to by the Senate.

It is perhaps significant that on this date, immediately after the Senate had passed the Joint Resolution, Senator Foraker, the author of both the Organic Act and the Joint Resolution, found it necessary to ask permission to print in the Record a very long defense of the Puerto Rican legislation in which he reiterated the high motives of the Republican Party and denied the existence of any differences between the original intent of the President with respect to the tariff question and the legislation as drafted and adopted.[4]

The House conference report was presented to the House on the same day, 30 April, and agreed to without more than an oral reading and no discussion at all. Perhaps the lack of discussion was due as much to the Republican Manager's statement when asking for its adoption as to the fact that no one had an opportunity to read the bill. Mr. Cooper, the Republican Manager, said:

(1) "There is no authority in the island of Porto Rico . . . , except only the military authority, which has been continued there until this time. The military occupation and military government, by reason of the law that has already been passed providing a civil government for Porto Rico, will cease to-night. Unless we take this action tomorrow morning there will be no duly constituted official in all the island of Porto Rico; . . .

"The purpose of this is simply to continue in authority those officials who are already there until the appointments provided for by the civil government act can be made. If you cut off the civil authority and cut off all other authority, I do not know what the consequences might be, but it does not seem to me that it admits of any argument that they would probably be complicated and serious." Sen. Foraker, p. 4853, *Congressional Record* Senate, 30 April 1900.

(2) ". . . and if the purpose of this bill is to limit the erection of new cane mills and sugar-making machinery to existing corporations, so as to create an additional monopoly under the guise of preventing monopolies, then I should object very strenuously to this or any other similar measure . . ." P. 4852, *Congressional Record*—Senate, 30 April 1900. Mr. Tillman.

(3) *Congressional Record*—Senate, 30 April 1900.

(4) Pp. 4853–4857, inclusive. *Congressional Record*—Senate, 30 April 1900.

"Mr. Speaker, this report is signed by the gentleman from Virginia (Mr. Jones), the Democratic member of the conferees, and I move its adoption."[1] The conference report was agreed to by the House and signed by the President on 1 May 1900.

III

The first attempt at revising the five hundred acre limitation contained in the Organic Act occurred in 1910 in response to a message from President Taft recommending the adoption of suggestions made in a report from the Secretary of War for needful changes in the Organic Act. The Secretary's report recommended a partially elective senate, a health department, a separation of legislative and executive functions, citizenship, a limited franchise, and a raising of the corporate land ownership limitation to 5,000 acres.[2] The Committee on Insular Affairs of the House, to which was referred the President's message of 29 January 1910 reduced the limitation to 3,000 acres in its version of the measure, H. R. 23,000.[3]

Although the bill was discussed and revised over a period of six months by both houses, relatively little attention was paid to the corporate land ownership limitation. It would seem from statements made by various members in Congress that sugar corporations had already acquired control of excessive acreages.[4] The restrictions against corporate land ownership in excess of the legal limit were greatly strengthened and drastic penalties added in this version.[5]

For the most part, however, discussion seems to have centered on the citizenship question which, in view of the fact

---

(1) P. 4884, *Congressional Record*—House, 30 April 1900.

(2) Vol. 80–B, p. 307–331, 61st Congress. Documents, Reports, Hearings, Act.

(3) *Ibid.*, p. 379.

(4) "There is one corporation engaged in raising sugar cane and manufacturing raw sugar, composed almost entirely of Americans and organized under the laws of an American State, and it is asserted—and whether or not it is true I do not know—that it is capitalized by money from Wall Street, that owns 30,000 acres of land in Porto Rico."

"There is another American corporation manufacturing sugar in Porto Rico, capitalized by money from New York, and, it is asserted, largely by the sugar trust. Whether or not it is true I do not know, but that corporation owns over 20,000 acres of land in Porto Rico . . ." Mr. Madison, p. 7624, *Congressional Record*—House, 8 June 1910.

"How dull has grown our sense of justice when we can not only tolerate monopoly, but now even legalize it! The ultimate aim of the sugar interest is obvious; for it is a fact that some of the companies have already, by circumvention and in violation of the spirit of the present laws, secured control of from 20,000 to 40,000 acres of this sugar land for each company, and it is now urged by the representatives of the sugar interest to permit each company to own from 12,000 to 15,000 acres of the land. I think that the restriction to 3,000 acres, the amount provided in the bill, is the utmost limit that should be allowed any company, and I sincerely trust that the safe-guards contained in the bill to prevent the acquisition of a larger amount will prove effective for that purpose . . . . ." Mr. Helm, p. 7628, *Congressional Record*—House, 8 June 1910.

(5) Pp. 8206–8207, *Congressional Record*—House, 15 June 1910.

that the Republican Party platform had promised citizenship to Puerto Ricans,[1] may have been the principal reason for the bill. In spite of Administration and Puerto Rican support, however, it was allowed to die in Committee.

The second attempt at amendment throws very little light on motives and pressures at that time. It occurred in 1917, with the introduction of a bill (H. R. 9533) to provide a new Organic Act for Puerto Rico. Although the five hundred acre restriction was not specifically included, the bill contained a general provision which would continue the limitation unless it were in conflict with other provisions.[2] However, the record reveals very meagre reference to the subject. The only person who displayed any real interest in the matter was Senator Broussard of Louisiana. His interest was in preserving the restriction and providing for forfeiture of excess holdings; but he capitulated on the latter after a rather weak effort at suggesting its insertion in the proposed bill.[3] The sponsor of the bill in the Senate, Senator Shafroth of Colorado, indicated that he believed that the limitation should be raised and that forfeiture was too drastic a penalty.[4] However, he professed a willingness to compromise and Senator Broussard did succeed in having an amendment inserted which specifically continued the five hundred acre restriction, called for a report to Congress from the Governor of Puerto Rico on all land holdings used for agricultural purposes, and reserved the right of Congress to legislate further on the

---

(1) P. 8179, *Congressional Record*—House, 15 June 1910, Jones.

(2) "Sec. 59.—That all laws or parts of laws applicable to Porto Rico not in conflict with any of the provisions of this act, including the laws relating to tariffs, customs, and duties on importations into Porto Rico prescribed by the act of Congress entitled 'An act temporarily to provide revenues and a civil government for Porto Rico, and for other purposes,' approved April 12, 1900, are hereby continued in effect, and all laws and parts of laws inconsistent with the provisions of this act are hereby repealed." P. 1328, *Congressional Record*—Senate, 13 January 1917.

(3) P. 1328, *Congressional Record*—Senate, 13 January 1917.

(4) "I am perfectly willing, when the matter is reached in the consideration of the bill, to have it amended in some particulars, but not to the extent of the stringent provisions which are contained in the Senator's amendment. I believe that the ownership of a certain quantity of land should be allowed: that it ought not to be limited to 500 acres... I believe that they should have a fair quantity of land there on which to raise sugar cane . . . and to fix the limit in this case at 500 acres, which is an insufficient quantity of land to enable a company to raise sugar cane, . . . seems to me would be an improper restriction . . . Another objection is that the Senator's proposal embodies the idea that there shall be forfeited to Porto Rico all lands which have been bought in excess of 500 acres . . . Those who acquired the lands have paid full value for them . . . So I want to suggest to the Senator that instead of providing that the land be forfeited to Porto Rico, by which the owners would lose them absolutely, they be required to dispose of those lands so as to get them in individual ownership, in order that the evils that might result from excessive holdings of real estate may be avoided, without the severe penalty of forfeiture to the Porto Rican government being inflicted . . ." Pp. 1328-9, *Congressional Record*—Senate, 13 January 1917.

subject.[1] This was later revised by the conferees of the House and Senate to call for a report on holdings in excess of five hundred acres and omitting the provision for further legislation. The bill was passed and became law in that form.[2] In all the eight or nine months during which the bill was being considered by Congress, there were scarcely 2,000 words for the printed record on the subject of the five hundred acre restriction—and these were not revealing.

Laws for the regulation of any industry are not likely to be useful throughout four decades; and the attempt at enforcement of this particular restriction after forty years was indignantly and repeatedly referred to by defense lawyers, when court actions began, as "persecution". For American capital, without regard to the prohibition, had flowed steadily into the new Possession and a great deal of it had been invested in agricultural enterprises of far more than the legal size. And there was no effective objection. It is not possible in a report of this kind to do more than suggest the reasons for this wholesale violation of the law. It must, of course, have been on the advice of counsel. It is difficult to believe that these aggregations of capital did not have good reason for feeling safe, for accepting the theory that the law was a dead letter and would never be enforced.

IV

Aside from the time-consuming efforts to uncover the theory which governed legislative history, there stood out, even in the preliminary study of materials available, what

---

(1) P. 3006, *Congressional Record*—Senate, 10 February 1917.
"That nothing in this act contained shall be so construed as to abrogate or in any manner impair or affect the provision contained in section 3 of the joint resolution approved May 1, 1900, with respect to the buying, selling, or holding of real estate. That the Governor of Porto Rico shall cause to have made and submitted to Congress at the session beginning the first Monday in December, 1917, a report of all the real estate used for the purposes of agriculture and held either directly or indirectly by corporations, partnerships, or individuals. That the right to legislate further upon this subject is reserved to Congress."

(2) "Senate amendment No. 75, page 44, is agreed to with an amendment. It provides that nothing in this act shall be construed as abrogating or in any way changing section 3 of a joint resolution approved May 1, 1900, with respect to real estate holdings, and directs the Governor of Porto Rico to have made and submitted to the next regular session of Congress a report of all the real estate used for the purpose of agriculture and held either directly or indirectly by corporations, partnerships, or individuals. The managers on the part of the House, believing that the report required in this amendment would entail a large amount of work and considerable cost upon the government of Porto Rico, and that every reasonable purpose and object to be attained can be accomplished by limiting the report to holdings in excess of 500 acres (since subsequent to the enactment of the joint resolution of Congress referred to no corporation engaged in agriculture could secure a charter which did not restrict it to the ownership and control of not to exceed 500 acres of land), have insisted upon such a limitation. The Senate conferees have agreed to this limitation. There are now some 55,000 holdings of agricultural lands in Porto Rico, the vast majority of which are of small acreage." P. 4166, *Congressional Record*—House, 24 February 1917.

25

was evidently a very deep-seated and still unsettled controversy. This had to do with the question whether large scale operations were necessary in the sugar industry, and particularly as it had developed in the Island of Puerto Rico; or whether it was the kind of activity which could be carried on by small, independent farmers. This was a controversy which anyone who knows the history of our agriculture will recognize as almost a universal one wherever monoculture is practiced. It is as prevalent in cotton, wheat, rice, perhaps corn, and certainly beef cattle, as it is in sugar. The small farmer through his legislative representatives has always contended that the factory-farm was not only a threat to his own economic interests but was a menace to society in the same sense that the trusts were evils in other forms of industry. In this controversy farmers were supported by all the members of the agricultural hierarchy who have grown so numerous and so powerful in recent years. It is, of course, an old theory that a sturdy peasantry is the most secure base on which to build a nation. Its modern proponents avoid the word "peasant" and talk largely of the "family farm" and of the virtues of land ownership, independence, and free enterprise, escaping from all objective tests and resting finally on a moral absolute. Anyone, I think, who comes to consideration of agricultural technique without the prejudice so often shared by those who have come under the influence of the various agricultural colleges, the Extension Service, and the Department of Agriculture, must certainly be puzzled by the character of these arguments. Farming is spoken of not as a business but as a "way of life", and exposure to the round of farm duties as somehow a more praise worthy regimen than the activities of city folk. The actual development of agriculture, however, seems not to have been greatly influenced by these moralistic considerations. Wherever it is suitable, the factory-farm has displaced the family unit and even in areas in which one-crop agriculture is impractical, the tendency has been toward the consolidation of farms into larger units and toward bringing even these under common management. In other fields of industry, the long trust-busting campaign did not prevent consolidation; it only called more intensively on the ingenuity of lawyers and financiers. In agriculture the concerted attempt of preachers, teachers, government, and credit agencies had a similar result. Large scale agriculture rapidly extended itself in all one-crop areas throughout the first four decades of the century; and even showed a tendency to establish itself in such mixed farming states as Iowa and Illinois by way of group management under bank or insurance company ownership. But everyone deplored it.

It appeared from the study of the materials available that Puerto Rico offered nothing more unique than an excellent specific illustration of the one-crop system and that whatever strictures had stood in the way had had the same effect as elsewhere. Even the law, apparently so rigid and hortatory, had been completely ignored. It could be argued, and indeed it was, that the latter-day attempt to enforce the five hundred-acre limitation was merely a late attempt to turn backward the inevitable development of technology; and that even if it did not fail it must turn out to be costly, costly in the direct sense of increasing the expenses of production and so the price of sugar. This, it was argued by representatives of the several defendants, could have the result of driving Puerto Rico out of sugar production; competition with other areas where no such nonsense was contemplated would be impossible. This attitude of the sugar corporations was, of course, as absolutist as that of the family farm proponents. It left out of account the whole problem of absenteeism and the long record of abuses for which the corporations were responsible in Puerto Rico.

It did not appear possible to argue that the present attempt at enforcement arose altogether out of a theory concerning the benefits of small scale as contracted with large scale agriculture. It was that. But it was also more than that. There was a felt injury. A whole people had suffered wrongs and those wrongs had finally created champions who were not to be diverted from the attempt to right them. The Insular Attorney General who first found courage to attempt enforcement must have known the professional and political risks he took. Possibly he may have exaggerated the economic gains to be got by enforcement. Certainly most others did. For enforcement was undertaken by lawyers who knew little about agricultural technique and had but a vague idea of what might happen after the absentees had been dispossessed. The briefs show that they generally accepted the dictum of the agriculturalists that small holdings

27

were the desirable substitute for absentee ownership, without recognizing this as a *non sequitur*. The problems of ownership and of management were separate, the one being a question of technique in production and the other that of sharing in the product; but this was wholly overlooked in the first approaches to the problem.

This matter of rehabilitation in rural life was not exactly new to me. I had been through these controversies before and had indeed administered an agency which undertook on a considerable scale to ameliorate conditions among the rural disadvantaged. I had learned then how blind the orthodox could be and how bitter and determined were the defenders of the accepted theory. Arguments were beyond reason; but methods of defense were highly practical. These consisted in discrediting anybody who ventured to disagree. The policy which had evolved in my mind from long periods of controversy, endless discussion, thoughtful consideration, was a resettlement plan which attempted to maintain the efficiencies of large scale production and at the same time to appropriate the benefits for previously disadvantaged people. The difficulty with large scale production was, indeed, the corporate form, not large scale production itself, for the corporate form drained away all the profits for the benefit of those who participated neither in the work nor greatly in the risks of the enterprise. In the case of Puerto Rico much of the profit went to the mainland and so the injury was intensified.

The lawyers who engaged in the attempt to dispossess the sugar corporations were not unaware that there was more than one side to this controversy and not unaware of its complexities. But they were inclined to accept the orthodox view of a field in which they were not expert. They assumed that the only alternative to the present system was the substitution of one in which independent colonos owned and managed the land. They identified the corporation with the techniques used by its management and concluded too easily that small individual ownerships were the only alternative to corporate agriculture as it was practiced in the instances before them. Indeed, it was because of this naive approach, I began to think, that you, Mr. Secretary, may have had the doubts in your mind concerning the utility of the law which I sensed when we first discussed the matter; and it was per-

28

haps a perception of the complexities of these problems which led you to ask for informed advice. Because of my experiences with the Resettlement Administration earlier, and because I was finding in the materials immediately available another instance of the same controversy which had been so tormenting then, it seemed quite possible that throughout any attempt to clear up the administrative situation this controversy would stand in the background. That proved to be the case.

An illustration was in fact available among the materials first circulated to the group of experts. This was the case of the Lafayette estate taken over and reconverted by the Puerto Rico Reconstruction Administration as one of its efforts toward rural rehabilitation. I have already spoken of the fact that in the first Agricultural Adjustment Act a system was authorized in which processing taxes collected in Puerto Rico might be pooled for the general benefit of agriculture there. The Chardon Plan had recommended that one of the items in a rehabilitation program to be financed out of these funds should be the taking over of certain sugar estates and operating them cooperatively. When the PRRA actually got started, Lafayette, a going central on the southeastern coast of the Island, was purchased for this purpose and cooperative operations undertaken. For various reasons, which will be referred to later on, it could, after a year or two, be pointed to as a failure by capitalistic tests—which is to say that its gross expenses were greater than its gross income. That many of these expenses were chargeable rather to its position as an instrument of the state rather than to its function in production evidently meant nothing to those who shared in the decision to abandon the cooperative features of the enterprise. It was offensive to those trained in the family-farm tradition. It seems probable that they would have liked it even less if it could have been defined as a success rather than as a failure. At any rate, it was interesting to see the disposition which had been made of the lands. They had been turned over to large farmers, about sixty of them, chosen, by some method, from among 2,000 or more applicants. Even in a preliminary way, the history of Lafayette outlined the controversies and prejudices which we should encounter and the solution which would turn out to be orthodox. Not only I but others, however, were given pause by the unabashed selfishness represented by using the majestic powers of government to advantage no more than sixty out of the thousands who in one way or another were sharers in the Lafayette enterprise. It might be that they were no more than workers there, perhaps even casual workers, but the government owed them equal-handed treatment —even more, to be fair, than even-handed treatment, because of their past disadvantages and present low estate. The Lafayette solution might or might not turn out to meet one of the conditions which any solution, to be completely successful, must meet—that is to protect efficiency—but certainly it would not meet the important test of diffusing benefits among as large a number as was possible.

As to the first of these conditions—efficiency—there was some light to be had from considering situations which had arisen in other parts of the world. Practically always when revolt against great landlords had taken place, the naive solution of division into small or medium holdings had been chosen. This was legally the simplest, of course, but also it was invariably the most desirable politically. This was, of course, because those who hoped to share in the division were the supporters of those who, as members of the government, did the dividing. The officials merely did what they were put there to do. They got land for their supporters. There had never been a case in the long history of seizure and division in which efficiency had been maintained under the new system. The evidence was that in Russia, in Rumania, in Mexico, and other areas where agrarian revolutions had taken place, the costs of production had risen frighteningly. In the most recent case, that of Mexico, President Cárdenas had been so concerned by the failure of production that he had attempted in a somewhat different way what the Russians also had been driven to: the maintenance of large scale techniques with a new approach to sharing the benefits. That this attempt was being liquidated under President Avila Camacho did not argue against its necessity. It merely pointed to another victory for the orthodox who feared that an experiment might succeed if allowed to continue.

It seemed doubtful whether Lafayette, with the kind of arrangement which was established, would succeed even in maintaining efficiency; but it was even more doubtful if improvement in sharing the benefits would follow. For a preliminary search of the records revealed that independent farmers of the sort now to be established at Lafayette had refused throughout the Island to make collective agreements with organized labor and that their wage rates and hours of labor were less favorable than those contained in collective bargaining agreements with the large corporations. Lafayette, on preliminary examination, was certainly a far from clear case. The question whether it was a failure at all except in the mind of the prejudiced was an open one and the question whether it would succeed by the tests of efficiency and humanitarianism was even more open.

An even more illuminating analogy was discovered in these preliminary investigations. This was the disposal of the so-called Friar Lands in the Philippines. These lands were divided as a result of prohibitions similar to those written into the Organic Act of Puerto Rico and at about the same period—just after the Spanish American War. The prohibition, it is true, was not so drastic. The limitation in this case was three thousand acres. The difference in the two cases was that the prohibition was enforced in the Philippines as it never had been in Puerto Rico. From all that could be discovered in tracing the history of the division and sale of the land, there was no point of view from which the policy could be said to have succeeded. The efficiency of production was so reduced that even after four decades many payments had not been made and the whole matter was one which those who had sponsored it preferred rather to forget than to use as an illustration of successful social reorganization.[1] Ought Puerto Rican policy be shaped in exactly the same way? Might it not also be a failure not only from the

---

(1) There is a difference of opinion about this. The Philippine Bureau of Lands reports the policy to be a success and gives the following reason: "The purchase by the government of the large estates above mentioned and their resale into small parcels to their tenants and other qualified persons had contributed a great deal to the solution of the agrarian problem in this country as evidenced by the fact that after the same have been equitably distributed. . . . . these places that used to be the hot beds of social unrest and the cradles of radicalism are now the homes of many prosperous, happy and contented small landowners and independent farmers." To one familiar with the field this statement has the old ring of fervor but a characteristic absence of fact. It was contained in a statement by José P. Dans, Director of Lands, in response to an inquiry in March, 1941. Several years ago Frederick C. Howe was made an adviser on homesteading by President Quezón. Instead of contributing something constructive to the situation he justified and confirmed the policy of division of the estates into fee-simple small holdings. In May, 1940 an Act was passed by the National Assembly of the Philippines authorizing the President to acquire private lands (through purchase or expropriation) "for resale in small lots," providing for an agency to carry out the policy and setting aside funds and authorizing bond issues for payment. This undoubtedly fixed Philippine policy for the immediate future. The easiest and most popular way was taken—even if the most costly to the public in the long run.

31

point of view of the individuals who hoped to benefit but also from the point of view of government which hoped to improve the lot of Puerto Ricans? It seemed so, for the solution taken at Lafayette was precisely that which had been taken in the Philippines 40 years before, and was now thought to have failed.

Puerto Rico is now, as she has been for centuries, almost fantastically dependent on the cultivation, processing and sale of sugar.[1] The currently accepted estimate which puts the proportion of the yield of sugar at sixty per cent of her annual income is considered a gross underestimate in terms of the realities. It is literally impossible to plan any income for about a million and a half people if market for sugar in the United States should by some chance be cut off. Yet the access to that market is determined by a quota system which is more subject to lively competition than it would be possible to believe if debates on the almost annual sugar bills were not available as public documents. Anyone can see displayed there an exhibition of human nature at grips with an economic privilege which is gained or lost in an annual struggle. If Puerto Rico has not fared too badly in the division of benefits it is because of certain sympathizers in the executive and legislative departments who are not connected with sugar. Puerto Rican leaders and responsible officials are never unconscious that their quota may suddenly be diminished and the subtraction divided among producers in other areas, an action which would as certainly condemn many Puerto Ricans as though they were put into a concentration camp and deprived of rations. This background of uncertainty and helplessness creates on the Island an attitude which is at once fearful and defiant, a kind of neurosis which affects the whole people. It cannot be a matter for much surprise that there should be a long sustained determination among the more conscientious Puerto Rican leaders to find more economic security. One way to do this would be to discover ways in which the Federal legislature might be influenced favorably. Obviously the best way to do this would be to have such a change in status that Puerto Rico was represented there. This, rather than a demand for independence, is the characteristic attitude

[1] Not taking into account the defense construction which provides, temporarily, as of 1941, an income almost exactly equal to that provided by the sugar industry.

of the Island's people. But another way in which some certainty could be gained would be by bringing under local control those policy decisions concerning the sugar industry which have so often been made by the vice presidents of banks in New York and Boston. The unconcern of these officials for other interests than those of their principals is not an element of reassurance. And no Puerto Rican needs to be reminded of poverty among sugar workers. The five hundred-acre prohibition in the Organic Act, as it was used in the case which precipitated action, was more an instrument of the desire for home rule, and for a measure of security, than for the purposes, whatever they may have been, which the Federal legislature entertained in 1900.

A peculiar conjuncture of events made the years of the depression a time which could be seized by patriotic Puerto Ricans to make at least some gains in an unfriendly world. The terrible depression which had prevailed since the War in most of agriculture had generally affected sugar in much the same way as it had other kinds of agriculture, yet with a somewhat different rhythm. The deepened industrial depression after 1929, however, definitely weakened the corporations who were the traditional enemies of change in insular institutions. And when President Hoover and all he represented went down to defeat in the election of 1932 and the New Deal came to Washington, it was conceived that the New Deal might just possibly come to Puerto Rico, too. And, of course, it did, in more ways than one. The most important to note here was that, for the first time since the Organic Act was adopted, there was found the courage and honesty among insular officials, encouraged by the Secretary of the Interior and certain others in Washington, to attempt the task of enforcing the old limitation. Not that those Puerto Ricans who undertook the enforcement conceived it as an agricultural reform; they conceived it rather, as I have said, as an instrument in a struggle against unfriendly forces in the outside world. The prolonged legal and judicial subservience was coming to an end. Puerto Rico had found the talent and the independence to attempt economic liberation.

One of the excuses which had always been used to explain delay and inaction was the purely legalistic one that Congress had provided no means of enforcing its own act and that because of the peculiar status of Puerto Rico it was impossible for the local legislature to implement an act of the Federal Congress. There had, of course, never been but one way to discover whether that was true. The courts would always have given an answer if it had been insisted on but they were either not asked directly and so could evade the issue by lingering on irrelevant points, or they had, in various ways, avoided the submission of the question. It must be said also that the insular prosecuting authorities had never shown any great initiative in finding out, once for all, what could be done under the law.[1]

---

[1] It is not easy to say why no penalties were prescribed for violation of charter limitations on the holding of lands. Mr. Hirshberg suggests that the drafters of the Organic Act considered that they were preparing a constitution, and in constitutions penalties for forbidden acts are not traditionally mentioned. Mr. Guerra Mondragón who has been in charge of the 500-acre cases for the Attorney General and who is a compendium of knowledge on all the legal niceties involved, thinks no light is thrown on the question by any legislative history now available except some almost casual references to be found in the debates on the Philippine bill. It was introduced on 7 January 1902 as Senate 2295 by Senator Lodge (*Congressional Record*, p. 474). It was reported by the Committee on the Philippines 31 March 1902 (*Congressional Record*, p. 3446). It was debated 9 May 1902. Mr. Patterson (*Congressional Record*. p. 5966) made certain remarks which have relevance: ". . . .There is another matter, Mr. President. Under the law of nearly every State, corporations are prohibited from holding lands except such as may be necessary for the business of such corporations; and yet I venture the assertion that there can not be found five cases in the court reports in which a corporation has been attached for holding more lands than it was entitled to hold under its charter.

"I do not know of more than one case in which a corporation has been thus successfully attached and the reason is this: Only the sovereign itself can wage a suit against a corporation for holding lands in violation of its charter. A private individual will not be heard in a court, no matter in what form he appears, for the purpose of having a court declare that the holding of lands by a corporation is illegal. That has been decided by the Supreme Court of the United States in **National Bank** v. **Matthews**, 98 U.S. 628. Also in 14 Peters 122, in the case of Runyon v. Coster and in almost an innumerable number of cases by the different State courts. This is the rule upon that question: 'Where a corporation is incompetent by its charter to take a title to real estate, a conveyance to it is not void, but only voidable, and the sovereign alone can object. It is valid until assailed in a direct proceeding instituted for that purpose.'

"The impending danger of a judgment of ouster and dissolution was, we think, the check, and none other, contemplated by Congress.

"That has always been the punishment prescribed for the wanton violation of a charter, and it may be made to follow whenever the proper public authority shall see fit to invoke its application. A private person can not directly or indirectly usurp this function of government. Leasure v. Hellegas, 7 Serg and R. 313; The Banks v. Poitian, 3 Rand, Va., 136.

"So, though it were not true that three or four individuals may organize themselves into a hundred and more different corporations, and each corporation may take 5,000 acres of land, and some one man in the entire number may get nearly all the benefits, nevertheless, unless the Government itself should move against the corporation for violating its charter, in the amount of land it takes title to, the corporations would be permitted to continue in the enjoyment of all that they were able to secure . . . . ."
The House report on this same bill after it had been passed by the Senate said:
"One of the greatest needs of the islands is the development of their vast natural resources. For this purpose capital must be induced to go to the Philippines, but only under such circumstances and so controlled and regulated by law as to prevent their undue exploitation. It is believed that the sections of the bill relating to franchises are so carefully drawn as to thoroughly safeguard the islands and their people against corporate or private greed and yet at the same time to present inviting opportunities for legitimate business investment.

"The franchise provisions are substantially similar to those which were reported by your committee two years ago and enacted into law as a part of the legislation for Porto Rico, and which have proven so satisfactory in that island." (P. 6835, *Congressional Record*, 14 June 1902, Report No. 2496.)
In the debate on the bill Mr. Jones (Va.) made an interesting attempt to make this Philippine law conform to that of Puerto Rico:
"Mr. Chairman, I desire on page 72, line 13, to move to strike out the word 'thousand' and substitute for it the word 'hundred' so that it will read 'control not exceeding two hundred hectares.' Mr. Chairman, all I want to say in this connection is that the fundamental law of Porto Rico provides that corporations engaged in agriculture in that

34

Without calling attention to any one kind of dereliction, it is possible nevertheless to emphasize the main fact: sugar company lawyers had all these years kept their companies out of the courts or had succeeded in so turning their cases that the courts could evade the issue. After a bad start, the New Dealers in Washington gave more honest attention to Puerto Rico than had been the case in other administrations and, since they represented less sympathy for business interests and rather more for common folk, corresponding New Deal officials in Puerto Rico were given support in undertaking, through the five hundred-acre limitation, a renewed attack on absenteeism in the sugar industry.[1] To make a long story short, and far less agonizing than it was as it went on through several years and many disappointments, a case finally did arrive in the Supreme Court of the United States and the question at issue was finally and unequivocably answered.[2] The People of Puerto Rico could determine the tenure arrangements under which their land could be held. It was this final outcome of the legal struggle which precipitated the administrative question under exploration here.

V

These materials having been circulated to consultants and some discussion of the issues involved having taken place, it was determined in a meeting of the group that two sets of hearings ought to be held. The first of these would be used to explore the economy of the sugar industry, the utility of the five hundred-acre provision, and so on, after which

island shall not hold exceeding 500 acres of land. If my amendment is adopted, it will make this section correspond very nearly to the Porto Rican law, 200 hectares being very nearly 500 acres.''

Mr. Jones did not prevail. In the House the statement of the House Conferees was inserted in the Record. The following paragraph of that statement is significant:

''The Senate further recedes from its disagreement to the provisions of the House bill relating to public lands, and agrees to the same with an amendment reducing the amount of land to be held by corporations from 2,000 hectares to 1,024 hectares. The Senate has further agreed to the House provisions restricting the ownership and control by members of corporations, and corporations, of mining and agricultural lands, with additional stringent provisions limiting these holdings.'' (P. 7697, *Congressional Record*—House, 30 June 1902.)

In the House the conference report was agreed to 30 June 1902, *Congressional Record*, p. 7703.

The Senate agreed to the conference report on 1 July 1902, *Congressional Record*, p. 7739.

The President approved the bill on 1 July 1902.

But this bill, too, contained no penalty clauses.

(1) Among those to whom most credit is due are Mr. Benigno Fernández García and Mr. Miguel Guerra Mondragón.

(2) I deliberately avoid discussion of the legal history as not within my terms of reference.

35

more definite conclusions could be formulated. These would then be subjected to another hearing. Thus we might at first bring to bear all the knowledge available, and uncover the interests which were likely to ask consideration for their point of view, later going on to prolonged consideration. It was recognized that all this was a delicate matter, that an attitude of complete impartiality would need to prevail in the first hearing; and that, in the second, whatever principles were put forward would need to be drawn carefully from the evidence at hand, and even then, would need to be held in suspension for whatever changes might seem necessary as the result of new evidence. If, however, this could be done successfully, it seemed possible that ways might be found to go forward into the administrative tangle left by the lawyers, and at last a beginning be made. This procedure was approved by you, Mr. Secretary, and I went forward with the arrangements.

It was during this period that the first of many defections occurred in the personnel of the group. Mr. Benjamin Cohen was detailed to go to London with Ambassador Winant and Mr. Carl Robbins began to see that he would have to remain in Washington for Congressional hearings. This double loss made a difficulty which was repaired by the addition of Mr. Monroe Oppenheimer, then Assistant Solicitor of the Department of Agriculture in charge of the Farm Security Administrator's legal affairs and Mr. Henry A. Hirshberg, General Counsel of PRRA; if the special abilities and knowledge which Mr. Cohen and Mr. Robbins had been expected to contribute were lost, there were special gains from the new affiliates. It had begun to seem likely that the rehabilitation work done by PRRA might possibly be taken over by the Farm Security Administration. There were some difficult negotiations in the way and there was the general difficulty of switching work from one department to another which is never very easy. However, there was the practically settled fact that Congress would furnish no more money for PRRA and that therefore its only support in future would have to be found in its limited revolving funds. Difficult as a rearrangement of liabilities and assets might be, it was so obviously desirable that I thought no effort ought to be spared to bring it about; if it were at all successful the utility of associating counsel on both sides was obvious. I was consequently glad of the addition of Mr. Oppenheimer and Mr. Hirshberg.

In the meantime, the First Assistant Secretary having suggested that Mr. Leon Cubberley of the Solicitor's Office act as Executive Secretary, Mr. Cubberley had familiarized himself with the material at hand and learned the preliminary disposition of the group. With this knowledge in mind, he proceeded to Puerto Rico to look over the ground and to arrange for hearings. These were set for March 10–14, inclusive. His instructions were to advertise the hearings, to arrange time for all with legitimate material who wished to appear, to find a public place, and to make sure, if he could, that the appearances were representative.

By this time study of the legal situation had resulted in a certain amount of clarification in my mind. It seemed to be true, as I had feared, that the proceedings had been undertaken with a somewhat vague conception of the ways in which the lands might be disposed of, once they were taken from the sugar corporations. The fact was that in the case which was furthest advanced, disposition had been provided for by an insular act. The alternatives of public auction or expropriation were provided. For the purpose of liquidation, a receivership had been set up so that the heavy responsibility for interim management and for disposition lay with the court. There had not been, so far as could be determined at that time, any thought given to the problem of financing the sale of the lands. The lawyers in the Attorney General's Office were not so neglectful of subsequent difficulties as appeared at that distance. They had ideas concerning both of these problems. But they had not yet emerged into law and so were unknown to anyone in Washington. Not until later did misunderstandings of this sort clear up.

Consideration of these problems, together with the determination of the price which should be paid for expropriated lands, continued, for the weeks remaining before the first hearing, to be the center of our thinking and discussion. It was possible to conceive that the lands might be taken and paid for out of funds raised on the security of the lands themselves. This could be done through the sale of what, in effect, would be mortgage bonds. This had been the method taken in the disposition of the Friar Lands in the Philippines. It

37

would involve a guarantee by the insular government, of course, but that did not seem to offer difficulty. The bonds would be immensely strengthened, however, if there were assurances that the lands would be operated as efficiently in the future as they had been in the past. This was, however, desirable in any case; and consideration of this problem led to the formulation of a preliminary rule that whatever was recommended to be done should be controlled by the probability that it would result in a method of production no less efficient than that now prevailing. It was recognized that this might well be difficult in view of the clamor there would be for absolute ownership by individuals who felt themselves qualified and who would be supported by agricultural orthodoxy. Nothing seemed clearer, however, than that the division of the estates in this simple fashion would result in lowered efficiency. If this were true it meant that a search had to be begun for some method of large scale operations which should get rid of the incubus of corporate absenteeism and yet maintain an unreduced yield from sugar to be diffused among the people of Puerto Rico.

To this specific problem the group devoted itself in long hours of discussion and prolonged individual thought. As it turned out, this was very nearly the dominant theme of discussion, also, in all the subsequent hearings. Out of the discussions, I, as a special advisor to the Secretary, began to find taking shadowy shape in my mind an hypothesis which so far was purely preliminary but which proved to be useful as focus for information and ideas which later became available. This hypothesis was shaped by the necessities of the case which have already been stated as (1) the preservation of efficiency, (2) the wide diffusion of benefits, (3) the satisfaction of the revolutionary emotions which evidently governed Puerto Ricans in this matter. The recent history of sugar production in the Island had been such, also, that it contributed something to the formulation of this hypothesis. The industry had passed through a bad time in the 1920's. It had suffered in general from lack of foresight and intelligence, these lacks registering in the almost unopposed advance of several serious cane diseases and a number of wasteful practices which depleted fertility and contributed to the loss of soil. Other sugar areas, such, for instance, as Hawaii, had been wiser in this respect and had devoted a certain percentage of profits to research and control. The worst of these difficulties, that of spreading disease, was eventually, however, brought under control by governmental research which led to the introduction of disease resistant varieties and better field practices. In the early 30's the production of sugar began to increase rapidly so that by 1934 when the first quota system was applied, production had reached 1,113,000 short tons. The quota system was based, however, on a five-year history so that production in Puerto Rico was limited to considerably less than that of its latest year. The sugar producers had felt very much aggrieved at this and had continued to complain of the unfairness of the historical base. They were left, they said, with a certain percentage of land prepared for cane which now could not be used for that purpose; and indeed there was evidence in A.A.A. records that the division of land suitable for cane which was not used for it was roughly 60 and 40 per cent.

It seemed to me, therefore, in formulating a preliminary hypothesis, that there was at least 40 per cent of land formerly used for the cash crop and presumably flat and fertile which would be available for other purposes. Why not use this 40 per cent to satisfy the clamoring hunger for land ownership and preserve the other 60 per cent for some sort of large scale operations under public auspices—not necessarily government ownership, but certainly not individual holdings. My thought turned to the way in which we had set up certain plantation operations in the Mississippi Delta country, in Arizona and in California under the old Resettlement Administration when had now become the Farm Security Administration. These projects had gone forward and succeeded. They had given that agency considerable experience in managing this kind of enterprise. It seemed possible to think of the Farm Security Administration either owning these lands and leasing them or loaning the funds to associations which might own them, but in either case determining the conditions of management to insure efficiency. Government ownership would probably be rejected by the orthodox; perhaps any kind of collective operations might also be opposed. But there seemed no other way to spread benefits and keep efficiency than to try some scheme of this sort. These, after all, were the great considerations. Also, it seemed that such an arrangement might avoid the criticism of the field technicians of the sugar companies who had always said that their acquisition of land in defiance of the five hundred-acre prohibition had been motivated by a desire for uniform supplies of cane. The Farm Security Administration might make a long term contract not only with the association which borrowed its funds, but, as manager, with the central to furnish cane in certain quantities and of certain quality.

It was at this point that the idea began to take shape in my mind that what was needed here was not so much a report for your guidance, Mr. Secretary, or even a plan of action, as patient and painstaking negotiation of new arrangements. It would be necessary to intervene between the Department of Agriculture and the Department of the Interior; to attempt the regularization of land taking; to bring enforcement of the law into coordination with the funds which the Farm Security Administration might obtain for loaning to individuals or associations; and to see whether insular legislation could not be guided in such a way as to assist in these arrangements rather than to interfere with them. To this, when I put it before you, you fully agreed.

I resolved to see whether, in the few months at my disposal and in the limited time I could spare from my duties in New York, I could not bring about a situation among the various government agencies, both Insular and Federal, in which the five hundred-acre limitation could be turned to useful purposes. To do this it would, of course, be necessary to find a source of funds for financing the alienation process and equally necessary to find ways in which these funds could be used to increase the well being of the Island. This would involve, as I conceived it: (1) the picking up of PRRA's work by other agencies, probably the Farm Security Administration; (2) the persuasion of the Farm Security Administration to cooperate in setting up a new pattern of rural life; and (3) the persuasion of the Bureau of the Budget or whatever other Federal agencies were concerned to cooperate in the program. It would be necessary not only to gain the willingness of the Farm Security Administration but, if necessary, to supplement its regular funds for that purpose. I could see how, with regular work going on, that agency would be unwilling to undertake new tasks unless it had additional funds with which to work. This was a real difficulty since the agricultural appropriation bill in which its funds are provided was already well under way and of course included nothing for this purpose.

I began, in spite of difficulties I could see ahead, to have conferences with Mr. C. B. Baldwin. the Administrator, and some of his assistants. They were interested and sympathetic; moreover they suggested that a possible source of funds might be found in enlargement of the appropriation for their agency as it passed through the Senate. Their hearings had already been held in the House of Representatives and no extra funds had been allowed. There was a prospect, however, Mr. Baldwin informed me, of an addition not only to funds available for loan purposes but also for administrative purposes. It began to seem with all this good will and cooperation that something beneficial might result. I was somewhat concerned, however, about the possibility of transferring PRRA's work to the Farm Security Administration and inserting into a budget worked on in Congress an appropriation specifically for Puerto Rican rehabilitation. Congress had hitherto been unsympathetic to any special treatment for Puerto Rico; in fact, the per capita appropriations made to the Extension Service had been consistently cut down in the House so that Puerto Rico received less than half the proportionate funds which went to other areas. Considering the poverty in the Island and its need for agricultural advice, they ought rather to have been doubled; but the probable unsympathetic treatment of any suggestion of this sort made it seem desirable to depend, at least in the begining, on the generosity of administrative agencies rather than on argument before Congressional committees.

If the Farm Security Administration could take up rehabilitation work in Puerto Rico on the same per capita basis as it was carried on in other areas, that would be sufficient gain for one year and if then it could go on to implement the alienation of lands under the five hundred-acre limitation with a modest allocation each year in the immediate future, that would be as much perhaps as could be expected without going to Congress and making a special case. It was not impossible that eventually the whole matter would have to be taken to Congress as an issue no more than half settled in an Act of that body, and which needed further implementation; but this decidedly did not seem the time to do that. Be-

41

sides, some sort of legislation was being shaped up in the Insular Legislature. Mr. Luis Muñoz-Marín, who was an old acquaintance of mine and who had taken part in many conferences in the days when the Chardon plan was being prepared had, as the leader of a new political group, the *Populares,* won, in a recent election, control of the Senate, at least, and had become President of that body. It seemed possible that the five hundred-acre issue, which had been prominent in his campaign, might at last be implemented. The program to which he was committed in agriculture was a definite one whose prominent features were: (1) the setting up of a land authority to receive lands alienated under the five hundred-acre limitation; (2) the financing of this transfer by bond issues with the land as security; (3) the establishment of small homesteads; and (4) the setting up of proportionate participation farms.

These Insular proposals, on investigation, seemed to differ only in detail from the hypothesis which had been shaping up in my mind. I was doubtful whether an insular land authority of this sort could finance itself on the necessary scale; and I thought it probably would be guided by the theoretical orthodox pattern of agriculture; but it seemed possible that this program could be brought together in some way with the Federal one, the two supplementing each other and providing an effective attack. This was certainly something to be further investigated on the spot and worked out by negotiation. I thought, however that there might be no difficulty about that. I had already had a cooperative letter from Mr. Muñoz Marín and had answered it suggesting the possibility of molding the two programs into one. All these tentative conclusions, you will remember, Mr. Secretary, I laid before you at this time, suggesting that possibly the Land Authority set up by Insular legislation might acquire the estate lands and that the Farm Security Administration might furnish the funds with which individuals and associations might lease or otherwise acquire them. This, I thought, ought to support the bond issues; and it might go some way toward quieting the fears of the central operators lest their supply of cane might be irregular. The one difficulty with the Farm Security Administration, that Congress would probably curb any progress toward bettering the land pattern, and had already, in fact, forbidden it to purchase or to hold land,

42

would thus be avoided and the powers of both agencies used to good purpose. Your approval enabled me to go forward into this rather complicated situation with gathering confidence.

VI

We arrived in San Juan to hold the first hearings on the 4th of March and began immediate conferences with the Governor, with Mr. Muñoz-Marín, and with officials in the Attorney General's office. In my interview with the then Governor, Mr. Guy J. Swope, I discovered that he was not at all out of sympathy with the land program but was naturally curious and perhaps a little apprehensive concerning my relation to the whole affair. He was anxious to cooperate so far as he could with the *Populares* who were the dominant political party and their commitment to the land authority bill was fairly specific and complete. He felt that if such a bill were passed, it would be necessary for him to sign it. His relief at discovering that my idea was to cooperate with, rather than to supplant, Insular action was quite apparent and he at once agreed that if we could bring Federal funds and abilities to bear on instruments set up in the new land law that would be as good an arrangement as could be expected under the circumstances. We agreed not only to these principles but to mutual consultation in the future and I went on to interview Mr. Luis Muñoz-Marín.

The land law, Mr. Muñoz-Marín said, was in process of being shaped but he did not conceal his commitment to its specific features. That had been the kind of compaign he had made, and he very definitely hoped that I would not feel it necessary to recommend any action by the Federal Government which was not consistent at least with its principles and if possible in accord with its specific provisions. The question I had to ask him was, I said, whether his interest was in doing something for the landless farm workers and the impoverished small farmers or whether what he really wanted to do was something of advantage to the large farmers or *colonos*. · I was rather disappointed that I failed to get a clear statement from him on this point and also on a point which did not then seen to be so important as it later became; that was, whether individuals were to be treated in the same way as corporations so far as limitation on land holdings were concerned. In spite of my lack of satisfaction on these points, on others we found no difficulty in agreeing and I felt after my interview with him, as I had after the previous one with the Governor, that considerable progress had been made toward Federal-insular cooperation. Mr. Muñoz-Marín offered to cooperate in the hearings and made it possible for us to secure a public room in the Capitol which had an advantage over any private place.

Subsequent interviews with Mr. George A. Malcolm, the Attorney General, and Mr. Miguel Guerra Mondragón cleared up some of the points in the legal situation which had been obscure hitherto and furnished grounds for more optimism concerning the program than I had dare to entertain. It began to seem possible that the corporations might be put under some kind of protective receiverships to be taken over according to a schedule. In this way, the funds needed could be planned for and their use anticipated some time in advance.

It was in an atmosphere curiously devoid of hostility all around that the first hearings began. I made it perfectly clear at the opening that I should not let the sessions be used for anyone's political advantage, that no speeches should be made, that every appearance should be recorded and published afterward and that what we sought was honest advice in solving a difficult problem. The chief appearances were of four sorts: for the sugar corporations, of course, as the interests chiefly effected; for the workers in the industry; for the colonos or independent farmers; and for what was called the "public". Those who appeared for the corporations were largely the Puerto Rican managers. No principals appeared except in one or two notable instances and those not absentee owners. There were, however, no lawyers, for which I was thankful since what I wanted was to explore administrative possibilities exclusively; and I had had some dread of being drawn into long legal controversies.

What was said at these hearings, the discussions, the exchanges of opinion, the differences, appears at great length in the filed transcript. What is not necessarily suggested there, of course, is the atmosphere which prevailed. It seemed to be a genuine relief to the representatives of the sugar corporations that it was carried on quietly and with a desire for technical consideration rather than for political advantage. One or two attempts to make speeches by self-seekers were suppressed in the interest of establishing a co-operative climate. The general good will which prevailed did not, however, in the least obscure the main conflicts. There was, of course, an irrepressible antagonism between sugar corporations and those public officials who had set out to enforce the five hundred-acre limitation; and there appeared at once the almost equally important difference between those who spoke for the colono system and those who believed in some sort of cooperative or associational agriculture. This last in particular involved interesting reversals of the attitudes which might have been anticipated. The sugar technicians, who, it might have been thought, would defend private operations at any cost, were so clear in their minds as to the necessity for large scale operations that they appeared to be for preserving the integrity of the going enterprise even at the cost of approving collectives. This is not to say that they believed in collectivism but that they were stronger in their distrust of land division than in their antipathy to the cooperatives. For instance, Mr. Marcelo J. Oben, General Manager for Luce & Company, said, when questioned: "I mean to say that if the government is going to do exactly like Luce & Company is doing, they might be able to do it just as efficiently, but not if each individual with smaller units of land is going to operate by himself." And this point he reiterated.[1]

Pursuing this theory into one of its further implications, I asked Mr. Oben whether he were making a distinction between ownership and management. And his answer was that the problem had nothing to do with ownership, that the form of management was the important matter. "I am talking," he said, "about the large unit, regardless of how it is operated," meaning, of course, how it was owned.[2]

This colloquy at the first hearing with one of the most respected technicians of the sugar industry seems worth repeating here at somewhat greater length:

"Chairman: 'What you are talking about is the necessity for having one management covering an enterprise?'

"Mr. Oben: 'Well, that or the properties operated as one unit, which is the same thing.'

"Chairman: 'What I am trying to clear up is the question of ownership. This has nothing to do with who owns it, so long as it is operated?'

(1) *Transcript*, First Hearing, p. 73, p. 81.
(2) *Transcript*, First Hearing, p. 74.

45

"Mr. Oben: ·'So long as it is operated as a large unit.'

"Chairman: 'It could be owned by anyone or anyhow, so long as it is one unit?'

"Mr. Oben: 'Yes, sir, it could be owned by different people, provided that this ownership will look to one management.'

"Chairman: 'You are interested here in arguing for the integrity of technological control over the property as one unit?'

"Mr. Oben: 'Yes, sir.'

"Chairman: 'I just want to be perfectly clear about that.'

"Mr. Oben: 'In these large properties there are pumping stations that have cost up to $65,000. It is not possible to conceive that a small farm, I should say even of 300, 400 or 500 acres, could develop a pumping station of that type. That can only be done with a large enterprise having a lot of funds available, and that could cover a large area. If we·were to divide that water from that pumping station into small plots, because that might cover 1,000 or 1,500 acres, dividing that into fifty acre farms, it is practically impossible to distribute that water, which is delivered at a high point.'

"Chairman: 'Forgive me for interrupting you again. I want to get this perfectly clear. There seems to be developing as you talk the idea that the contrast of the operations now being operated by Luce & Company is the dividing of the farms into farms of fifty acres or more?'

"Mr. Oben: 'Yes, sir.'

"Chairman: 'There are other possibilities, of course?'

"Mr. Oben: 'Well, if the properties are divided into fifty acres or larger, are they still going to be operated as a larger unit?'

"Chairman: 'You are just talking on the point of management, which has nothing to do with ownership?'

"Mr. Oben: 'Yes, sir.'

"Chairman: 'But every once in a while what seems to crop up is that what you are opposing is dividing up farms into fifty acres. You don't want fifty acre management.'

"Mr. Oben: 'No, because I don't think it is profitable.'

"Chairman: 'You don't care if there is fifty acre ownership?'

"Mr. Oben: 'No, divided up in fifty acre plots. There are many other difficulties in dividing those lands. There is the question of roads and loading stations. If a lot of people have to load at one loading station, there will be great difficulty because sufficient facilities will not be available unless a large expenditure is made to provide those facilities for the small farms. There comes also the question of the farming equipment. A small farm is not in a position to have equipment large enough in relation to the size of the property.'

"Chairman: 'This is the same question again of overhead cost.'

"Mr. Oben: 'Yes, sir. In the operation of small farms, my experience is that people owning small farms would employ much less labor.'

"Chairman: 'Provided the operation were independently managed?'

"Mr. Oben: 'Well, yes, independent management. Of course, I am taking into consideration here that the lands are to be divided into small farms.' ''

.   .   .   .

"Chairman: 'Does that, to your mind, go some way towards showing what would happen if, we will say, the sugar property that you speak of were divided up into fifty acre farms?'

46

"Mr. Oben: 'Yes, sir.'

"Chairman: 'It doesn't have any bearing on what might happen, however, if the property were operated as a whole, or if the ownership were transferred, we will say to the government or to a cooperative association or anything else, so long as the integrity of the management were preserved?'

"Mr. Oben: 'If Luce & Company, in this case, is supplanted by a government institution, to operate exactly as Luce & Company, it should be exactly the same, if done economically and efficiently.'

"Chairman: 'This is a question of management and not a question of ownership. I want to make that clear.'

"Mr. Oben: 'If it continues to operate as a whole, as one unit. I should say that that . . . . . these figures, I don't want to use this 50 per cent increase, but only 20 per cent, and if that is applied to the 16,000 acres of cane that Luce & Company harvests every year, it would be a reduction of about 160,000 tons of cane, which would provide from 65,000 to 75,000 mandays, or equivalent to from ninety to a hundred thousand dollars that would not go into the lands of laborers.'

"Chairman: 'Or anybody else?'

"Mr. Oben: 'Or anybody else; but that is the fact; and that would mean that from 650 to 700 men would be out of a job for 100 days. That is my point of view, if these lands should be divided.'

"Chairman: 'In your opinion could sugar in Puerto Rico be produced at all under such conditions in competition with lower cost areas?'

"Mr. Oben: 'It would put us out of business.'

"Chairman: 'Puerto Rico could not compete with other areas?'

"Mr. Oben: 'That is my opinion. In talking about the amount of idle land, we have about 19,000 acres of land that is not in cane cultivation. It is all on hillsides and marshes and swamps. It is not possible to really cultivate anything on account of the dry condition, and it has to be used mostly for cattle.' "[1]

Here the argument ran off into questions which had to do with absentee ownership. But it will be seen that there was no question in Mr. Oben's mind about the necessity in Puerto Rico of maintaining the integrity of the relatively large-scale operation. The same point was made by Mr. J. M. Giles who represented Sucesión Serrallés. He wanted especially to insist, he said, "that the large farm produces much more income than the small one." And he had a good deal of evidence from his experience to put into the record. An interesting minor emphasis in his testimony was the prevalent habit among small owners of allowing the large operators to become their tenants. I had been aware of this and had often discussed it with Puerto Ricans. Sometimes it was

(1) *Transcript*, First Hearing, pp. 74–6.

ascribed to a Spanish distaste for labor and longing for urban gentility. But Mr. Giles thought the reason might be that the large operation was more efficient, obviously so:

"Chairman: 'What you are saying is that the small owner or independent operator is under a disadvantage which makes it difficult for him to compete, or shall we say, to operate at all, under the same conditions, as the larger operation?'

"Mr. Giles: 'He cannot operate as efficiently.'

"Chairman: 'Might this be the reason why in Puerto Rico there is such a large number of people who move off their land and move to town, leaving the sugar companies as tenants?'

"Mr. Giles: 'That may be the reason.'

"Chairman: 'That doesn't have to do with the character of the people? That's just common sense, isn't it, to go off and let some one else do it?'

"Mr. Giles: 'Usually they get a suitable arrangement, or a lease, and they go off and live on the rental and let the other fellow do the work.'

"Chairman: 'Is there any reason why this could not be done under the enforcement of the five hundred-acre limitation?'

"Mr. Giles: 'No. If all the land we own were divided up into five hundred-acre farms and they could be leased to us, we could continue as we do now.' "

But this led to some other considerations; and one of them had to do with where the profits were made—on the land or in the mill. I had suspected that opposition to the five hundred-acre limitation was more violent than was warranted by the reasons usually given—such, for instance, as the assuring of a steady supply of cane throughout the grinding season. I wondered whether the attachment to the land of A.A.A. subsidies was not a hindrance rather than a help. The first confirmation of this was Mr. Giles' testimony.

Another interesting conflict had to do with the clear testimony that the colonos were hard on labor. It appeared that collective bargaining arrangements were a regular feature of corporation operations but that no collective bargaining arrangements had been worked out with independent farmers, nor was there prospect of any, according to the representative of the Free Federation of Labor. Hours of work tended to be longer and wages lower, he said, on colonos' farms. It might have been thought that he unduly favored the corporations from his testimony on this point; but he made it very clear that he was not opposing operation of the land under other auspices, merely the forcing of a colono system in place of the prevailing one under which at least some gains had been made by labor.[1]

In this connection also it appeared quite clearly from testimony that if there were to be a division of lands into independently operated units, those units could not be expected to be much less than 50 acres.[3] Under these circumstances simple division yielded the information that with 175,000 acres to be divided, not more than 4,000 independent farmers could be set up. This certainly did not seem like the widest possible diffusion of benefits. Moreover questioning of most witnesses on this point produced substantial agreement that this was so.

On the whole, the hearings could be said to have been successful in the sense that they had produced quiet and careful consideration of the issues involved by those who were closest to them, and they were closed with all of us who participated feeling that those who had appeared, no matter how greatly they might differ, were really at one in wishing to further the welfare of Puerto Rico; and not even their own interests would be allowed to stand in the way of that. If the leadership could be furnished and the instruments devised, I felt confident that real gains might be made.

Most of those who knew most about the sugar industry and therefore gave the most technical information were, of course, employees of the sugar corporations and were therefore obviously prejudiced. Characteristically they began by saying that they were opposed to the five hundred-acre limitation. That, however, appeared to be more or less a formula and they were apt to go on from there with some relief to the discussion of ways in which the alienation might be carried out, if it were determined, after all, to do so. This discussion was often more technical than is necessary for elaboration here. It can, however, be found in the transcript which has been made available in mimeographed form. Perhaps the

[1] "Dr. Emerson: 'You have no agreement with the small colonos '
"Mr. Nogueras; 'The colonos have never accepted the invitation made by the Free Federation of Labor to come in and negotiate a collective agreement.'
"Chairman: 'Is there any actual difference between the wages paid or the conditions of labor established in the Association of Sugar Producers and the independent colonos ?'
"Mr. Nogueras: 'Well, there is a slight difference. Fortunately, the Federal determination of wages has compelled the colonos to pay the minimums established in our collective agreement, because the determination establishes almost the same scale of wages, and that protects the workers' wages throughout the Island. . . . There have been some complaints among the workers, but we have many complaints from workers working with the colonos." *Transcript*, First Hearing, pp. 19–20.

conclusion which stood out more prominently than any other, at least to my mind, was the sharp separation which these technicians were willing to make, when questioned, between ownership and management. It seemed to them, as it had seemed to me, in a preliminary way, that absentee ownership had reached such a stage of diffusion and remoteness that it could not possibly be more careful in its supervision than government is reputed to be. I could see no genuine distinction between overhead control by the agents of financiers in New York or Boston and the heads of bureaucracies in San Juan and Washington and I believe there is no distinction which has any genuine impact on the industry. Government, if that is any consideration, might be expected to be more humane and for that reason perhaps inefficient in a capitalist sense, because of distributing benefits at the time of work rather than much later in the form of relief; but that was not a distinction which ought to confuse reasonable people. The conduct of the industry would not be made less efficient in any sense by the substitution of officials for financiers. And indeed the sugar technicians very clearly feared the division of land into small holdings far more than they did a change in ownership.[1]

VII

Following the hearings, the various members of the group returned to their respective duties in Washington and elsewhere and I, as Chairman, undertook to formulate, in accordance with the prearranged program, a series of principles which should form the basis for the second set of hearings. These were circulated to the members of the group and discussion resulted in their considerable modification. It was suggested to me by others of the group that my attitude was too rational and too forthright and my lack of consideration for agriculturalists' prejudices was too marked. It was my feeling that this was the time for the utmost candor, for solutions which were directed toward the success of a new program rather than toward salving orthodox feelings. Nevertheless I was overruled and the statement which I had prepared was considerably modified. Mr. Menéndez-Ramos was genuinely

---

[1] Most witnesses who appeared not only submitted to questioning without evasion but handed in memoranda, usually prepared with considerable care. These were carefully collated and are available for study with the trnscript. Often the testimony in the transcript refers to these memoranda and all the points referred to are there more extensively developed.

convinced that the colono system was the only one which would succeed technically and the statement as finally adopted represented a considerable compromise on his part. Mr. Robbins believed that nothing short of permanent government ownership of the land as a preliminary to the use of government credit in setting up enterprises would do. Mr. Monroe Oppenheimer and others felt that, as a matter of technique, other means could be worked out for gaining the same objectives. It was their contention that the recommendations looking toward greater cooperation, more participation by government, would result in labelling us Communists or something of the sort and discrediting the whole proceeding; nevertheless, the set of principles which were published as a basis for the new hearings suggested the need for admission to the benefits of the land of a far larger number of Puerto Ricans than the colono system would allow.

There were eleven points in this statement. It follows.

1. The United States Supreme Court has held that the Legislature of Puerto Rico may determine, within the limits of the 500 acre restrictions, how the policy of Congress is to be realized. This policy restricts corporations engaged in agriculture to the ownership and control of not over 500 acres of land.

The 500 acre limitation, in express terms applicable only to corporations, does not go far enough and the division of 500 acres regardless of value, use, or productivity is obviously arbitrary. The limitation does, however, provide a useful means for approaching a wider diffusion of benefits from the soil and for lessening the prevailing sense of exclusion from the land. Literal enforcement is to be regarded as the beginning of its enlargement in such ways as will advance the welfare of the people of Puerto Rico.

2. This enlargement has recently been undertaken by the Insular Legislature. The Land Law of Puerto Rico, recently enacted, establishes a Land Authority to acquire the holdings of artificial persons in excess of 500 acres. But it imposes no limitation on the amount of land which may be held or acquired by individuals. This and other changes in the Law would seem necessary if it is to be useful in attaining its expressed objectives. The all important consideration is to have effective administration of the facilities provided by Insular legislation or made available from other sources.

3. Because the sugar crop is vital to the economy of Puerto Rico, and the Island is already a high cost area, maintenance of efficiency in production is imperative. For this both large-scale working areas and scientific crop and field management are essential.

4. The most generally acceptable land tenure pattern, assuming unlimited land, would be individually owned and operated family-type farms. That pattern has traditionally symbolized security and independence. It should be followed where conditions of soil, rainfall, and topography do not make large-scale agricultural operations imperative. To assure any considerable diffusion of benefits, however, individual holdings should be limited to genuine family-size units, with such restrictions on alienation and seizure for debt as will assure tenure and forestall reconsolidation into larger than family-type units. Individual family-type farms cannot now be established in large numbers. To do so would be to reduce yields and to increase costs. Highly intensive farming is made necessary by the scarcity of land.

3. One suggested alternative to family-type farms is for natural persons to buy excess corporate holdings in large units or to lease them with option to purchase. This would not fulfill the spirit of the law. It would transfer to a few the incomes of present corporate owners, with no adequate assurance that present efficiency would be retained or that whatever gains may have been made from collective bargaining would be maintained.

6. A better procedure would be to provide for initial holding by a public agency, setting up on family places, with secure life-time tenure, as many families as possible who desire to live that way, and establishing cash-crop farms to be operated on a participating basis. With continuous and active supervision of farming practices, present efficiencies and yields should be retained. This would leave open for the future the possibility of eventual family ownership or any other tenure arrangement which may in time be evolved as especially suitable for Puerto Rico. These arrangements ought finally to be worked out by the people of Puerto Rico.

52

7. Action by Federal agencies, assuming satisfactory tenure arrangements, should center on financial assistance based upon supervised farm and home plans.

8. Valuation of properties to be acquired ought to be determined without regard to governmental benefits.

9. The alienation of lands now controlled by corporations which also operate centrals will make necessary a thorough study of the future relations of centrals with the suppliers of cane. The objectives should be fair payment to growers and an assured sequence of supplies to the centrals.

10. Education, health, and housing policies must be restudied to meet the new conditions of agriculture and to develop subsistence activities. Changes ought to be made looking to wider diffusion of benefits resulting from the Sugar Act of 1937. Assistance from the A.A.A., the S.M.A., and the N.Y.A., should also be sought in stimulating insular subsistence crops and in raising the nutritional level.

11. Planning, coordination, and the following-up of execution ought to be centered in the Governor's Office under the direction of the Division of Territories and Island Possessions and the Secretary of the Interior.

During the course of the discussions leading to the adopting of the eleven points, I again had occasion to confer with you, Mr. Secretary, on what was being done and again had your approval for the procedure. It was at this time, too, that you permitted me to go forward with the negotiation of an agreement between PRRA and FSA by which FSA would in future assume responsibility for rural rehabilitation and for a resettlement program, and PRRA would withdraw, turning over its assets and liabilities to the FSA. Once this agreement had been made and initialed by Mr. George Mitchell, Assistant Administrator of the FSA, Mr. Miles Fairbanks, for the PRRA, and Mr. Hirshberg, Counsel, I felt more than ever confident that my plan of negotiating a program into being was going to succeed. There was very evident, among the officials of the FSA a growing perception of the Puerto Rican problem and a very satisfactory sense of responsibility. After all, Puerto Ricans were very much like their clients elsewhere.

At this time, also, I conferred at some length with Mr. Harold Smith, Director of the Budget, as well as with others of his staff, in order that the Bureau of the Budget might be informed of the proposal for a transfer of responsibility and funds. I found these officers helpful and sympathetic and felt that no objection was likely hereafter to come from that agency. This, of course, had to do more with the program of rural rehabilitation than with an enlarged program of land-taking which would be necessary if all the estate lands were to be liquidated within any short period. It was my feeling at this stage, however, that if a program of resettlement and rural rehabilitation could be got well under way, the land taking, which would be incidental to it, might well be large enough to go as fast as was feasible in taking the sugar estates. There was a good deal still to be worked out, of course, in the way of coordination of the Attorney General's program in Puerto Rico, of provision of funds, and the setting up of management devices, but that would necessarily have to be a continuing negotiation between a new regional officer of the FSA and the Attorney General's office in Puerto Rico.

There was, however, by now, a new factor in the situation. During all the time the group was in Puerto Rico the land authority law had been under discussion. Its various drafts were studied by all members of the group and the drafters had had opportunity to confer with us. Nothing in the draft, however, came from us so far as I am aware. And certainly nothing was volunteered from our group. The law was not actually passed until after our return to Washington but preliminary copies of it were available as we studied the agenda for new hearings. It had not been changed in essentials from what we had hoped it might be, although in certain respects it was defective as an instrument through which the Federal Government might use its credit facilities. To begin with, it left out of account all individuals and was aimed at corporations. This was more a psychological matter than a practical one because only corporations had been named in the Organic Act of forty years before; but it was feared that this might be interpreted as somehow anti-American since most of the corporate capital came from the continent and most of the individual holdings were Spanish. The argument on the other side was that it was perhaps a larger program than could be carried out in any foreseeable time if only corporate lands were alienated and this was

54

perhaps true. And yet an estate owned by a corporation was in exactly the same economic situation as one owned by an individual.

A greater difficulty was the preponderant dependence on the so-called proportional benefit farm which FSA had no powers to implement since it could not itself purchase land but could only lend to individuals or cooperatives. This device seemed to be neither. This and certain other technical defects were not ones which were irremediable and amendments might be expected to correct them before many operations had been undertaken. However, Governor Swope had signed the law and it would become effective on the 12th of July after which there would be a Board in Puerto Rico called the Land Authority which would have considerable powers to carry on the negotiations which I had undertaken. I hoped that some strong man might be put at the head of this so that what had been begun might be finished up effectively. As the time approached for the second hearings which were set for May 26–28 inclusively, Messrs. Emerson, Hirshberg, Duggan, and Oppenheimer withdrew from the group for various reasons beyond their control, leaving of the originals only Mr. Mitchell. For Mr. Oppenheimer and Mr. Hirshberg, Mr. Harold Starr was substituted, a lawyer from the Solicitor's Office in the Department of Agriculture familiar with the operations of the FSA. The advice and counsel I had had from all of them, however, had left me with the main outlines of a solution. There remained only the modifications which might come from the hearings and, as I have tried to indicate, the continuing of negotiation, so that the end result might be an established condition rather than a literary effort.

The second hearings produced nothing astonishing in the way of information but they served to publicize the new approach to the land policy and prepared the way for the operations of the Land Authority when it should be set up a little later. Aside from this, they served to expose an amazing concurrence among the agriculturalists who were unanimously determined to establish a pure colono system. There was unblushing admission that this was not in the interest of the people of Puerto Rico but only of a small group of already well-to-do farmers. But it began to seem that this might not prevent the Land Authority from finally adopting the principle. It was and is a very powerful sentiment and to go against it takes courage; but at least an alternative was suggested.

The appearances at this hearing were mostly the same as at the first; that is to say, they represented the same interests. The sugar technicians as a rule approved Point 6, which suggested the shaping of some kind of pattern to preserve large scale efficiency, even though they deplored, as before, taking the lands from the sugar corporations. This last, of course, they were bound to do.[1] There was even more indication that it was possible to conduct central operations without ownership of contributory lands, a point which the sugar corporations had denied with great tenacity until the time of the hearing.[2] Many ways in which separation could be made successful, and indeed had been made successful, in other areas, were outlined. As to the operations of the Land Authority which would be set up within a matter of months, there was considerable expression of misgiving, largely centering around the word "politics."[3] This perhaps arose from political uncertainty in Puerto Rico, and the widespread feeling that neither the best men nor the best system are chosen for the tasks to be done by bureaucracies but that everything is shaped to the advantage of a few. It would remain to be seen, of course, whether the Land Authority would make a competent record and the confidence of its supporters seemed to be based rather on the fact that its own financing would be rather limited at first. For myself I thought that for the most part it would depend on funds furnished indirectly by the Farm Security Administration whose record in respect of these matters had been excellent and could be

---

[1] See for instance, the testimony of Mr. R. A. González, etc., etc. In this connection, a significant suggestion was made by Mr. Manuel A. Del Valle, Director, Association of Sugar Producers of Puerto Rico, that the removal of American capital might jeopardize the market for Puerto Rican sugar. This point deserves consideration: Proportional profit farms, he said, would help to build up anti-American sentiment in Puerto Rico and this might lead to a resentment strong enough to have economic consequences. "The ousting of continental American enterprises from the Island is one of the greatest mistakes that can be made. The advantageous position that the Cuban sugar industry holds at present over Puerto Rico is not due, in my opinion, to any greater love for Cubans from our continental brothers, but to the fact that a much larger proportion of sugar in Cuba is owned by American capital . . . I believe that the day that American capital is denied the privilege to establish itself in Puerto Rico all of Puerto Rico is going to suffer for it." *Transcript*, Second Hearing, pp. 81–87.

[2] The statement of Mr. Acosta Velarde, a greatly respected technician of long experience was valuable on that point. (See *Transcript*, Second Hearing, pp. 56–68.) Also that of Mr. Francisco Colón Moret, agronomist, of Central Lafayette. (See *Transcript*, Second Hearing, pp. 68–78.)

[3] Mr. López Domínguez, in a thoughtful discussion, went on to suggest that while a division of profits had been provided for, a division of possible losses had been overlooked. He also felt that a wide distribution of benefits was not being contemplated and suggested modifications looking in this direction. As between individual small farms and large-scale enterprises, he felt that both ought to be allowed for and cited technical reasons to support his contention. (See *Transcript* second hearing pp. 101–6.)

expected to bring to the situation the same efficiency it had exhibited elsewhere.

It was not possible to discover what the attitudes of the principals in the sugar industry were. In this, as in the former hearing, they had chosen to be represented by local managers, they themselves keeping in the background. This was, of course, consistent with their usual policy. An incorrigible attitude of resentment against absentees is prevalent in Puerto Rico and for reasons which are easily understood. They take care to appear but seldom in public and are represented only by lawyers and managers. There had been a number of subterranean approaches made to see whether I would have private conferences, to which I had always responded in the negative. I ought to report, however, that I did have a meeting with Mr. Penfield Dudley who, though he presented no credentials, I was assured by third parties whom I trusted, really represented at least some of the important investors. I told Mr. Dudley that I felt the one best thing the owners could do was to appear in person and for once be frank with the public and the other interests involved. I said that I should be resentful if lawyers appeared at the hearings but not if sugar managers did because from them administrative technique could be learned. Study of both transcripts will show that practically no owners chose to appear in public but that my desire concerning the absence of lawyers was respected. In view of the choice made by those who felt that their integrity required a veil between themselves and the public, I thought it well to say, in closing the second hearing, that such irresponsibility was inconsistent with the privileges they held and that I felt their conduct in every way reprehensible. If the results in the long run should not be to their liking, I implied that they would be able to find no one to blame but themselves. This statement of mine, which received considerable publicity in in the Press, was however, like all the rest, received in a kind of bitter silence by the owners who evidently expect to be protected from rough handling by public officials and to be able to negotiate in the back rooms of the banks.[1]

---

(1) ''I must say . . . that it has been the source of some chagrin to me that so few (owners) have deigned to appear. I think it is no violation of confidence to say that a number approached me privately . . . I invariably told them nothing could be done privately in a matter which so closely touched the public interest, and I see nothing unseemly in putting it in the record here. I feel that there has been a complete sense of irresponsibility on the part of ownership . . . This is not intended as criticism of their representatives who have appeared here and who have given us the benefit of their technical advice.'' *Transcript*, Second Hearing, p. 205.

The closing witness at this hearing was Mr. Luis Muñoz-Marín, President of the Senate and leader of the *Populares*, to whom reference has been made hitherto. He entered on the record a brief explanation of the Insular law and some defense of it, expressing confidence in its operations and making it clear that he hoped its operations would be so gradual as not to disrupt the economy of the Island.[1] Under questioning he denied that there was anything anti-American implied in not making the law applicable to individuals as well as to corporations.[2] I myself had hoped that individuals would be included, not retroactively but as to the future, and I felt and do feel that there is no excuse for not doing it. In numerous conferences with Mr. Muñoz-Marín, Mr. Guerra Mondragón, and others who drafted the law I have put my point as forcibly as possible and have met with only one answer: that there is enough to do with corporate lands without including individual lands as well.

VIII

After the close of the hearings, in pursuance of my desire to leave accomplishments rather than merely a report in your hands, I negotiated further arrangements between representatives of the Farm Security Administration and of the Attorney General's Office, looking toward a coordinated program for the furnishing of funds and of bringing corporate holdings into receiverships ready to be taken over. These have progressed to the point of informal agreements which will be found noted in the file to be turned over to you. I have every confidence that, with the progressing operations of the Land Authority, these coordinated arrangements will work out satisfactorily. This is perhaps the matter for greatest satisfaction in the whole enterprise.

After my return to Washington I again initiated exchanges and conversations among all those associated with the group who could be reached and a new statement was

---

(1) *Transcript*, Second Hearing, pp. 194-202.
(2) He did not directly attack the problem. His statement was rather general, and could even be called evasive. It left me, at least, unsatisfied: "I never heard that extreme hunger and poverty was American, and certainly under the New Deal it would be less so. . ." This referred to an article by Mr. Everett Wilson, a representative of the Sugar Producers Association, which had been published in certain Continental newspapers. Mr. Wilson's aspersions on the un-Americanism of the *Populares* was not restricted to the selective enforcement of the 500 acre limitation. He made a number of other points as well. And this general condemnation gave Mr. Muñoz-Marín his theme. It was well taken and well argued; but it had nothing to do with the immunity of individuals as against corporations from the restrictions of the Act. *Ibid.*, p. 202.

drawn up, as the official act of the group, which met with substantial agreement of all concerned. That statement follows:

Since the Joint Resolution of Congress of May 1, 1900, corporations in Puerto Rico engaged in agriculture have been restricted by their charters to the ownership and control of not over 500 acres of land. Nevertheless, and despite reaffirmation of this restriction in the Organic Act of Puerto Rico enacted by Congress in 1917, various agricultural organizations, some admittedly corporate, others of debatable legal status, have acquired and control extensive properties

No change has been made in the Federal law establishing this land policy of Puerto Rico, despite attempts in Congress over 20 years ago to enlarge the permissible acreage to 3,000 or more. It is apparent from the Congressional debates that the 500-acre limitation was motivated by a desire to prevent a land monopolization under which a few large corporations might dominate the Island's agricultural development. Granting that the policy was conceived at a time when small-scale agriculture was of a greater comparative efficiency than at present, and that the limitation at 500 acres regardless of value, use or productivity is arbitrary, the limitation must be accepted and recommendations must be predicated on the assumption that it will continue to be the law.

The law was ignored and regarded as a dead letter until 1935, when the Puerto Rican legislature made explicit provision for its enforcement by quo warranto proceedings. In upholding the validity of this legislation, the Supreme Court of the United States has said:

"Surely nothing more immediately touches the local concern of Puerto Rico than legislation giving effect to the Congressional restriction on corporate land holdings. This policy was born of the special needs of a congested population largely dependent upon the land for its livelihood. It was enunciated as soon as Congress became responsible for the welfare of the Island's people, was retained against vigorous attempts to modify it, and was reaffirmed when Congress enlarged Puerto Rico's powers of self-government. Surely Congress meant its action to have significance beyond mere empty words. * * * As the ultimate legislative guardian of the Island's welfare, Congress confined the legislature's discretion within the limits of the five hundred-acre restriction. How this policy was to be realized was for Puerto Rico to say."

Seeking further to implement the policy, the Legislature of Puerto Rico, by an Act effective 12 July 1941, established the Land Authority of Puerto Rico, with power to acquire the holdings in excess of 500 acres of "artificial persons" engaged in agriculture. Included in the definition of "artificial persons" are private corporations, limited companies, partnerships, voluntary associations, Massachusetts trusts and other organizations which continue to exist regardless of changes in the persons participating. The Act declares as unlawful the acquisition, holding or any other form of direct or indirect control of land in excess of 500 acres by any "artificial person". This legislation is now under attack in the United States District Court of Puerto Rico. For the purpose here, however, it will be assumed that if the challenged Act is nullified by the courts, it will be followed by other Insular legislation seeking similar objectives as an incident to enforcement of the 500-acre limitation.

Unquestionably the difficulties of enforcement have been increased by the passage of the many years during which both Federal and Insular authorities ignored the existence of the limitation, and large corporations and their innumerable stockholders, by reason of this inaction, acquired what they regarded as vested rights. But these difficulties can be overcome if they are met with patience, tolerance and good will.

Whether or not absentee investors of capital and the managers of their estates in the Island have been moved by a desire to exploit its natural and human resources is irrelevant to the problems incident to the enforcement of the law. It is true that a substantial part of the Island's income from sugar is taken out of the Island; but it is equally true that part of the income will go out of the Island in interest if Federal Government financing takes the place of absentee private capital. The fact, which may be conceded, that large-scale operations under the present system have probably reached a higher productive level than any substitute system is likely to develop, is less important than the vast democratizing movement which the 500-acre limitation represents; that movement can no longer be ignored. The present system has failed to democratize industrial processes; it results in an ever narrower participation in management and income.

The ends to be sought are these: Satisfaction of the home-hunger now so generally frustrated; participation in the yield of the land by the largest possible number of those who labor on the land; compensation for those whose interests under the present system are affected by the establishment of the new system; preservation of the Island's sugar economy which might well be lost if the cost of production should be unduly increased.

For practical attainment of these values there should be:

(1) Effective legal procedure to break up all holdings of more than 500 acres, whether by corporations, by ''artificial persons'', or by individuals [1] who now are affected by neither Federal nor Insular limitation.

(2) The appointment by the Insular Supreme Court of receivers with authority to operate the properties until arrangements for their valuation and eventual transfer can be effected.

(3) Establishment of a Land Authority (already provided for by the Insular law now in litigation), with power to acquire and to dispose of land and to borrow money on its security.

(4) Expansion of the functions on the Island of the various Federal agencies, so that they may finance and furnish education and health services for families employed on, or who may acquire, lands from the Authority.

(5) Assurance of uninterrupted supply of necessary cane for efficient mill operations throughout the grinding season; to this end, growers might authorize the Land Authority, or other appropriate agency, to make contracts on their behalf with the mills. Or some form of public utility status might be devised which would impose regulation on all parties to these contracts.

The land and management pattern largely dictates the human associations to be established. The most generally acceptable pattern would be individual family type farms on which the families would have the security of tenure traditionally associated with ownership, an opportunity to achieve independence, and a decent standard of living. However, many—if not most—of the farm laborers on the lands in question now lack the technical and managerial skill required for

---

[1] R. Menéndez Ramos would not extend the law's operation to individuals.

successful operation of individual units, and for the coordination of such operations necessary to obtain the benefits of present day technology. For this reason, and to avoid disruption of the sugar industry, subdivision of present large-scale holdings should proceed cautiously. If lands are acquired by the Land Authority before subdivision is practicable, consideration should be given to the efficiency of going managements. The present staffs should, wherever possible, be retained; their knowledge and competence have brought the sugar industry to a high technological level, and this ought not to be impaired. They could be utilized either directly by the Land Authority or as lessees of proportionate profit farms provided· for under the Land Authority law. However, lessees of such farms should not be permitted or required to operate on the basis of speculative profits, should not be allowed to become owners of more than 100 acres and should not be selected or retained on a political basis. In all this, individual family type farms, with their operations effectively coordinated, should be kept constantly in mind as the most generally desired goal whether owned or leased, provided the social interests in conservation, etc., are guarded.

The suggested procedure is for gradual acquisition of estates over a period of years with a definitely spaced program so that all involved may know what to expect and so that transition may be as smooth as possible. The first step, as each increment is taken over, should be mechanical reconstruction and planning by the Soil Conservation Service. Rehabilitation loans by the Farm Security Administration should be made available, on the basis of supervised farm and home management plans, as available funds and supervisory personnel may permit, and full use should be made of the credit and supervisory facilities of the Farm Credit Administration. Work and retraining centers should be established by the National Youth Administration or the Insular Department of Education or both. The Insular Department of Health should establish health centers. In this regard, care should be taken not to lose the many advantages to workers which have come from various welfare schemes already introduced by the more enlightened managements. The office of the Governor, acting for the United States Department of the Interior and as the Insular Executive, should be the active coordinating agency responsible for drawing up a plan and for following it in execution.

The following valuation procedure would seem desirable: the Land Authority Law should be amended to authorize the appointment by the Governor of three Commissioners, the chairman of which should be technically qualified. The findings of this Board should be reviewable by the courts; their compensation should be included in the Land Authority budget. Valuation commissioners should exclude governmental benefits from the values they establish.

It is recommended that the United States Congress be urged to return to the system first authorized of pooling benefit payments to Puerto Rican sugar producers and expending them through appropriate agencies for the general benefit of agriculture in the Island.[1]

RUSSELL LORD,
CARL ROBBINS,
HENRY A. HIRSHBERG,
R. MENÉNDEZ RAMOS,
MONROE OPPENHEIMER,
GEORGE MITCHELL,
R. G. TUGWELL.

---

[1] R. Menéndez Ramos would have some limit on this, excepting smaller producers.

61

It will be recognized that any statement on so complicated a matter which would be agreeable to a number of people would represent a good deal of compromise one way and another. And this one was no exception. Into it went, however, an immense earnestness on the part of all my collaborators together with the distillation of their years of experience. The compromises were less serious than might be imagined. Somewhere along the line, we had lost Mr. Duggan, for what reason I do not know. He simply stopped answering communications and did not attend the second hearings. The A.A.A. has always been something more than simply orthodox as you are aware. It has tended to represent the most well-to-do farm opinion. Mr. Duggan represented its Southern region. It is not too hard to guess, therefore, why he thought it best to withdraw from any exploration of the land-holding system in Puerto Rico. It has obvious implications for the South. Yet while Mr. Duggan was with us none of our conclusions had seemed to shock him and his interest in the problem was obvious.

It remains to recall some of the relevant happenings which followed. For one thing I was made Governor of Puerto Rico, partly through your intervention, and was confirmed by the Senate after a rather severe examination which I shall forward to you for the light it throws on Senatorial attitudes and my own, both in the matter of land policy and Puerto Rican affairs generally.[1]

Such a hurried colloquy as goes on in a Committee room, and the cross-examination atmosphere which is apt to prevail, does not lend itself to thoughtful formulation of conclusions. Yet in such a situation half-held opinions may suddenly crystallize. I find as I read over my testimony that it became quite clear to me when I actually approached the issue that in Puerto Rico universal land ownership by the government would be unnecessary, and because of well established prejudice, undesirable. Certain of my colleagues would perhaps not agree with this; and I should modify my own statement in certain respects. But in general, and in view of the opposition to anything "socialistic", I would far rather see something established which was collective or cooperative but which would protect the general interest in the

(1) The transcript appears as *Hearings Before the Committee on Territories and Insular Affairs, United States Senate, Seventy-Seventh Congress. First Session on the nomination of R. G. Tugwell as Governor of Puerto Rico. U. S. Government Printing Office.*

conservation of soil and water. And I believe that some such solution would be best. Small home places in private ownership; cash-crop farms in regulated collective ownership— if this could be done all the values sought in reorganization might be gained.

I do feel that some rather extensive promotion of new crops by the government can only be done through State farms. This is for technical reasons. What is needed above all in Puerto Rico is new hill crops. They exist now on the experiment stations; but they need to be brought to what, in industrial research, is called the pilot-plant stage. Quinine, teak-wood, the mahoganies, various grapes, certain bamboos which are resistant to termites, many plants which bear essential oils and others which are the sources of insecticides, improved citrus varieties, certain promising fibre plants—these and many others need to be planted now on the thousand acre scale. Among them will be found, I am sure, what is needed: substitutes for the tobacco and coffee which are declining, the one because of erosion, the other because of hurricane damage and market failure. But until the new crops have been demonstrated on a plantation basis they cannot go into wide production. Immense risks are involved, and a long time, in growing tree crops. And no individual can afford to experiment with them on an adequate scale. But this is not necessarily to suggest government ownership as the only solution of the tenure problem. Government ownership is objectionable to the orthodox. I myself have no feeling about it one way or the other, if it should promise to be instrumental in gaining what is needed: efficiency in production, diffusion of benefits, conservation of resources, and security of tenure. All these, it will be seen, can be gained in other ways than through government ownership, though it is often pointed out that these are not the simplest ways. Concerning that, I long ago discovered that elaborate and sometimes expensive devices are necessary to save face for the orthodox when a change is needed. This appears to be one of those situations. The most difficult conditions to bring about are conservation and security. The fee-simple ownership system, without regulation but with free mortgage rights, has ruined about half the land of America and most of the hill lands of Puerto Rico. A man who owns land will not—and then later cannot—take measures to prevent erosion and loss of fertility. The old idea that this kind of owner-ship leads to the best use has been refuted on an extravagant scale. I still hear it said in the face of billions of wasted funds and millions of gutted acres. But I do not have to believe it. I only have to recognize that others believe it against all reason.

The same thing is true of security. Everyone familiar with American agriculture must know that the most haz-ardous situation possible to a man of family is to have the fee-simple ownership of land. At the first adversity he seeks a mortgage; thence through tense and tortuous stages he descends to tenantry. And it is not a tenantry of a re-spectable and recognized sort. It carries the stigma of failure. In the best counties of our richest farming states sixty to seventy per cent of the farms are operated by tenants. These again are vast and solid facts which, if they mean anything, certainly mean that ownership is hazardous. But the dangerous element in it is the pledge of land for the loan at interest beyond the normal earning capacity of the land. This too can be prevented by means short of govern-ment ownership.

Those of us whose hearts are wrung by the ills of farmers exploited in these ways and expected to preserve a public interest in their enterprises for which they are not paid, are willing to take any road forward. We are not dogmatic. In Puerto Rico the hill lands can only be rehabilitated by new cultures undertaken at considerable risks running through a generation. Individuals alone are not equal to that challenge. Only by working together and with public credits can such a program be carried out. But that might mean a new concep-tion of loans without interest for 20 or even 40 years on the security not of the land but of the crop and with supervision of the practices by the government.

As for the great cash crop, sugar, I feel that the colono system will probably not succeed if brought into competition with other areas where monoculture on a large scale is practiced. Consequently, I had rather see the present estate system kept intact but with a change in ownership. This ought to involve participation in benefits by all who work there, not merely by a few. The colono system restricts benefits rigidly and by diminishing efficiency reduces their total amount in any case. People who argue otherwise point

64

to the assistance which comes from agricultural colleges, experiment stations and the extension service. But they do not add the cost of these in the colono bookkeeping. It was in recognition of these facts that the suggestion of proportional profit farms was made and embodied in the Land Authority Act. Perhaps that device will work. Certainly Puerto Rico is not the best place in which try a collectivization which depends on the sharing of judgment among many workers. That could only succeed at a far later stage of developmenr.

Meanwhile it has fallen to me, as Governor, quite unexpectedly, to name the members of the Land Authority and its Executive Director. For membership on the Authority I have chosen a Geographer, Professor Rafael Picó; a sugar technician, Mr. Acosta Velarde; the Dean of Agriculture, Mr. Rafael Menéndez Ramos; and, by arrangement, Mr. Ralph Will who is Regional Director for the FSA. As Executive Director I have called back Mr. Carlos Chardon from three years of expatriation in Venezuela. These, together with the Commissioner of Agriculture, are the men who will work out the policy for the new system in Puerto Rico. I shall, of course, follow their work closely. And from time to time I shall report to you what progress is made or what failures have been experienced.

I am, Mr. Secretary,

Respectfully yours,

R. G. TUGWELL.

LA FORTALEZA
December
1941

65

Pearl Harbor was still three months in the future when Mr. Tugwell relinquished the chancellorship of the University of Puerto Rico (to which he had been elected by the Board of Trustees during the summer and which he had assumed on 1 August) to assume the Governorship. Yet he already foresaw what must come, sooner or later, to the island. In his inaugural address as Governor he said he would soon call a special session of the Legislature to devise some way to control rising prices and meet the perennial problems of Puerto Rican life. He joined, he said, "in the campaign against the two enemies of all mankind: poverty and slavery."

INAUGURAL ADDRESS
SAN JUAN, SEPTEMBER 19, 1941

FELLOW CITIZENS:

At the outset I must express the general gratitude of everyone to Dr. José Gallardo, my immediate predecessor in this office, and through him, if I may, to those many other Puerto Ricans who have held it—sometimes for extended periods. A number of those men are around me today. I think the only pride I have on this occasion is in their goodwill If I should ever lose that, I should not care to hold this office. I shall never preside over a dangerous division of Puerto Ricans of which I am in any way the cause.

What can a Governor of Puerto Rico say on his inaugural day? He is not yet fully aware of his responsibilities; he has not yet tested the capacities of his office. He cannot therefore forecast much in detail what he will do. He can, however, express his sense of dedication to the duties which lie ahead and point out certain of the problems to whose solution he will turn first.

My own desire to be of use to Puerto Rico is not a new one, nor did my attempt to serve her begin just yesterday. In this respect I can only say that I will go on as in the past. Some of my hopes for the future I outlined a few weeks ago, when I addressed the students at the University. I did not dwell then on the problems. That, I thought, I ought to do today. But as I reflected on an obvious list of them it seemed to me that there was one beside which all others sank into insignificance; which, if it could not be solved, made all others insoluble. That was the problem of poverty. On that, I thought, it would be more than seemly to dwell. It would be cowardly not to recognize its existence. Justice cannot be founded on a farming and working folk who live at the level of a million or more of our fellow citizens in Puerto Rico. It is useless to expect the full development of higher things under such circumstances. To look for the growth of the arts, for a University in which philosophy is the center of interest, for wide-spread cultural and recreational facilities, for the production and publication of literature—all this kind of high human aspiration seems thwarted and hindered in the presence of extreme misery. To walk in the streets of cities and be confronted with a slum; to travel through the

69

countryside and to see everywhere the huts of the landless: these facts must press upon the conscience of every sensitive person; so that the first task to be undertaken is the bettering of these conditions. To it I have the right to ask Puerto Rican leaders to give their best energies until real accomplishment has been made.

It is not a task which is impossible—if it be given devoted attention. The solutions — the theoretical solutions — have been pointed out often enough. Poverty is not merely the result of a mechanical relationship between the resources of a region and the number of its people. On either side of such an equation there are infinite possibilities of variation: the resources may be of many kinds, more or less wanted by the world outside, more or less useful as means of subsistence at home, more or less available, actually, to those who have to depend on them for support.

The people may differ greatly, too; not, I think, in intelligence, for that seems to run constant through all races and classes in all lands; but certainly in helpful custom, in energy, in organization. There may be a general attitude which approves class division and even a fatalistic attitude toward privation. Or there may be held out to every man opportunity to use his talents; and there may be resentment at any limitation on these rights. Energies may have been wasted in the fatal downward spiral of underproduction and malnutrition. Or there may be fortunate factors. Sunshine may supply an otherwise deficient intake of vitamins; diseases may be limited by immunity; there may be a prevailing temperamental courage which is a real even if imponderable factor.

As to organization: this is perhaps most often the source of difficulty. It is at once the most stubborn and, with resolution, the most easily remedied limitation on progress. It may be devised with a view to control by a small class and to limiting the numbers of that class. There is no hope when such a situation exists and sooner or later something happens: either the ruling class gives way voluntarily or it is in some way made to share its privileges with others. In contrast it may be that the system is a democratic one in which opportunities are opened to all who have ability; in which the good things of life are shared with generosity; and in

70

which there is such a measure of security for the individual as can practically be attained.

To bettering the condition of the poor I shall bring every resource I am able to find in the Governorship. I will be the friend of every man or woman who helps; I will be the opponent of every man or woman who hinders. Whatever needs changing for this purpose must be changed; whatever is useful must be fully employed.

I am aware of some, at least, of the circumstances which will make my task easier and some of those which will make it harder.

There have been developed here only a limited number of products for which the world is willing to pay; and of those one, which can be grown in large part more economically elsewhere, has a predominance which, if inevitable under the circumstances, is nevertheless dangerous. Furthermore, the goodwill of continental neighbors is necessary to its market, a goodwill which sometimes falters in the stress of competition. No way out of this one insecurity has ever been suggested except the doubtful expedient of trying to become altogether self-sufficient. This is certainly not possible, not even in the United States as a whole; but it is still true that we may by earnest effort and the acceptance of certain risks develop other products and activities of importance. To do so it is only necessary to realize clearly the natural elements at our command. Of these elements the most important is the soil; but there ought not to be neglected a sun which shines nearly every day in the year, rain which falls upon our mountains freely, a wind which blows with regularity—a whole climate, indeed, which ranges only from good to better. We have no coal or oil; but sun, wind, and water will be the important sources of power in the future. We have a deficiency of arable land by present standards; but what if its productiveness should be doubled or quadrupled? Would anyone, in view of what has happened in the past two decades, question such a possibility?

If sun, rain, and wind give us power for factories; and the land yields raw products to be converted there, what then becomes of that favorite frightener, overpopulation? Certainly, it cannot truly be said that this island is overpopulated so long as its resources have not been fully utilized and brought to the people. If its agricultural and industrial

71

organization has not been well calculated to develop the highest efficiency in the interest of all, no one knows what progress might be made with better organization. The responsibilities put upon us by the fertility of the people must be met with plans for greater production. There is nothing wrong with our children. The trouble is that we do not feed enough of them well in infancy, teach enough of them to live and work with efficiency when they are young, and provide them with opportunities and security when they are grown. These are failures of leadership, of ingenuity and of generosity. And it is no escape from this conclusion to charge fertile families with irresponsibility.

This does not imply that society should forego its interest in encouraging increase among the healthiest of its citizens and discouraging increase among the obviously unfit. But it does suggest that the easy alibi of overpopulation which excuses neglect, lethargy and selfishness is not one into which we should allow retreat without challenge.

On the question of social organization there are great possibilities. I am, of course, not prepared to say what arrangements will best fit the circumstances of this island in the future. But I can see that a homogenous people, two million in number, on 3350 square miles, much of which is mountainous, need, in agriculture and industry, the best of leaders, of managers, and of technicians. They cannot afford speculators and profiteers. The time is past when absentee capitalists can expect to extract extravagant percentages of gain, using the people's need and their own monopoly to force the acceptance of usurer's terms. To the other kind of capital—investment—we can offer the security of our basic riches, certainty of return, and the good faith of a government which has never broken its word. But that kind of capital will appreciate the absence of speculation and concentration on the tasks of production.

What is the way into this future? Through constant improvement in administration, through research, through education, through the work of a deepening social conscience. The sources of all these can be established in the University. But if those sources are to be made amply useful, the University must find closer and more intimate relations with industry, with agriculture, with government, with the suffering and hope of our people. The theory of an institution set apart on a little island of scholarship, ignoring the confusions of the world must be given up. There individual ambitions must be transmuted into effort for the common good; there technical excellence must be created and turned to the combatting of poverty, disease, and the inefficiencies which lie behind them.

I do not hesitate to point out that there are controls older than any government and even more closely associated with the guidance of individual action. The institutions of religion once were the dominant influence in preparing young men and women for adulthood. I have noticed that the secularizing of this ceremonial is often associated with stress among youth on privileges rather than on duties. The body of ancient wisdom entrusted now so largely to the schools is certainly imperfectly administered. The scepticism of science is good for approaching technical problems; but it leads to chaos when universally applied in social affairs. If we are to depend on the consciences of free men to produce justice and order, there must be well-agreed references of honor. From their support men of the church must not turn away; and others must not neglect to ask help from this oldest of sources.

In bettering public health, in educating children, in bringing power, light, sanitation, into people's homes, in building more homes for the underprivileged, in providing all kinds of needed public works, in the conservation of soil and other resources, in replanting forests, in the use and tenure of the land, in the search for higher wages and greater social security—in all these we shall find work enough crowding upon us in the years to come. We must not avoid any of it. We must bring to bear on the tasks to be done all the resources we can find of administrative ability, good judgment and energy. And the incompetent and the unwilling must be kept from hindering the efforts of others. We cannot afford to ignore the fact that our system is in competition with others for the favor of the world. To talk largely of freedom, of security and of individual rights without finding ways to translate these words into action will no longer suffice. The test has come, and it is a test of performance.

While the totalitarian armies are in the field their propaganda offices at home never cease to deluge every continent and every island with claims of superior efficiency. They are able, they say, to offer better order and even higher living levels. Those claims will be suggestive to our own under-privileged in proportion to their disappointed aspirations. The totalitarian propaganda has the advantage of being altogether in the future, of not being tested. We however, cannot be vague. Whether we are really doing what others say they would do is a matter of fact to be observed by anyone. It is fortunate, from this point of view, that there lie behind us some nine years of effort. Much has been accomplished, more begun: public works, assistance to farmers, fair play for workers, better health services, earnest efforts at soil saving; and finally, of course, the enormous task of helping to save democracy.

As an instance of the special actions we must take to carry on this work, I shall issue a call for a special session of the Legislature to deal with two emergencies: inflation of prices and the provision of new water supplies and sewerage systems. About these matters I shall have more to say. For the moment I only insist that all our farmers and workers have gained in increased employment and higher wages shall not be lost through rises in the cost of rice, beans, and the other necessities of life; also, that water supplies, in some parts of the island, which have never been safe and now are so inadequate as to give only part-time service and sewage disposal systems which are are so primitive as to endanger public health belong to an age in the past. Both are remediable deficiencies and they ought to be made good at once.

These are immediate; but there are other facilities which must be enlarged and multiplied, other arrangements which must be perfected. Hindrances may arise. They must be removed. I shall not hesitate to ask the Legislature to meet whenever necessary to carry out the people's program. There must be no question in any mind of our resolve to use all the resources of government not only to insure freedom but to create plenty.

Puerto Rico is a good testing ground for American intentions; I am sure her leaders realize quite clearly their role in the great drama which is unfolding. Not only is this island by size and location the strategic center of the whole Caribbean area, it is also joined in culture with other Americans to the South and to the North. If Puerto Ricans will make the attempt, they can be responsible for establishing such institutions of international friendship as have seldom before existed. It requires full realization and forthright effort. But if it succeeds, the nations of this hemisphere will owe to Puerto Ricans a debt they will proudly acknowledge for years to come.

I think I can speak for the people of the States. They would say to you who are their fellow-citizens that their union with you will never be allowed to become an unwilling one. For this moment in the world's history we are jointly committed to a great struggle for freedom and decency. When the kind of international organization has been insured in which federations of nations can exist in safety, the people of Puerto Rico will perhaps canvass again what is in their hearts with respect to our common citizenship. I can predict that this is an issue which will be settled only among Puerto Ricans, and that the conclusion will be wholly respected.

Meanwhile I join you in the campaign against the two enemies of all mankind: poverty and slavery. As we succeed, we shall earn a place in the world's counsels and in the hearts of people everywhere.

The Japanese had two months more of treacherous preparation to do before they would be ready to strike. The special session which the Governor had promised opened on October 23. Prices were still going up, and the Governor's message had a word of warning that merchants could not expect to do business as usual in wartime. His opening paragraphs emphasized the source of Puerto Rican staples rice, beans and codfish. They came from outside and could not be controlled by the island itself. Congress was still debating price control in the States, so he advocated an Insular O. P. A. until the Federal government could catch up. He spoke of taxes, and proposed the planning of public works to prevent wide-spread unemployment when war construction dropped off. Above all, he said, there·was no point in fighting for democracy abroad if we were not willing to try to make it work at home. He spoke feelingly about the island's inefficient administrative system.

MESSAGE TO THE LEGISLATURE
SPECIAL SESSION

Senators and Representatives of Puerto Rico:

I

Some time ago, the then Governor, Dr. Gallardo, impressed by the difficulties imposed on working people by the evident rise in prices, appointed a committee to investigate. The reports of that Committee have amply confirmed the ordinary observation. In the basic food-stuffs, price rises of 20 to 30 and even to 50 per cent have not been uncommon. These have more often been rises in wholesale than retail prices, but in retail prices, too, there have infrequently been what appears to be unjustified increases.

It is not necessary to say that profiteering is taking place. It is more accurate to say that in a situation such as we face now the ordinary motives of business must be modified in the public interest. What is considered usual in ordinary circumstances, becomes improper in time of national emergency. At such a time the dangers and sacrifices are regarded as ones which all ought to share and from which no one should be exempt.

What the Governor's Committee found was that the ordinary processes of business were resulting in great sacrifices by the consumers of staple goods and considerable and unusual gains by those who dealt in them. Such a condition does not appeal to the conscience as justifiable, and naturally some remedy is sought.

In seeking this remedy, there ought to be as little disturbance as possible in the courses of trade; but at the same time no measures ought to be neglected which will secure equality of sacrifice among all members of the community.

What measures are available to secure such a result?

The problem of inflated prices is very simply expressed by saying that it is a condition in which goods are relatively scarce and money is relatively plentiful. In the present situation both these elements are present and are growing in importance. The nation's productive facilities are being turned to making defense goods and away from making

79

consumers goods; there is more volume; this increases employment and consequently wages. But the increase in volume of goods is not of commodities purchaseable by private consumers. People, who before have not been able to supply themselves and their families with certain kinds of goods or with sufficient quantities, now have the funds; but this occurs at a time when the goods are less available. They are bid up. Both producer and middleman profit by this competition amongst consumers to spend money. And they have to be prevented from doing it. There is no objection to legitimate margins, but no one has a right to take advantage of a national crisis for private advantage. So far as unwarranted increases by producers is concerned, that is a problem which, as has been indicated, for many widely used products, is beyond Puerto Rican control. Rice, beans, codfish—the great staples—come from outside. Primarily their prices must be a Federal problem.

Remedies can theoretically be applied at either end or in the middle. All are being advocated at the moment. Wages could be decreased. But that would put an end to our traditional way of encouraging effort and is therefore undesirable. Consumers goods could be increased, but that would jeopardize the defense effort. Apparently whatever remedies are used have to be of less simple sorts.

It is possible to withdraw part of the new volume of purchasing power involuntarily through taxes. Funds thus withdrawn can be put into reserves to be used when defense work ends and unemployment is again increasing. This, if it can be done efficiently, has the effect of transferring purchasing power from the present, when it is a threat, to the future, when it will be a boon. Suggestions have been made of taxes considerable in percentage. These ought to be considered carefully.

It is possible to regulate prices: regulation can be either at wholesale or at retail; if at wholesale, there is the risk of unchecked increases by retailers; if at retail, the danger is that so expensive a policing organization will be necessary that much of the benefit is lost. This has to be taken into account.

It is possible, also, to establish equitable prices by "yardstick" methods. For instance, rice, beans, dried fish, and certain canned foods could be distributed through controlled stores, with administrative methods much like those used for certain surplus commodities, but limited to the amounts and periods necessary to the desired effect. If this could be done economically, it might be an effective check.

I mention these possibilities more as showing that it is not necessary to accept as inevitable a situation which is harmful to our people than as specific recommendations of what to do in the circumstances. And this is true even if no action with local effect is taken by the Administrator of the Office of Price Administration and Civilian Supply in Washington.

The inflation of prices has been a matter of concern to the Federal Government almost since the passage of the Lease-Lend Act, when productive facilities began to be transferred to the uses of war and at the same time incomes available for the purchase of goods became greater. In an uncontrolled economy a scarcity of goods with an increase in purchasing power will always cause prices to rise. But from such a situation only certain classes in the community gain. Others lose. And the community itself loses because what goods there are go to those who have the most money, not to those who need them most or those who are contributing most to the national effort.

In such situations some measures of control are always taken. In this crisis the President, using the powers given him by Congress when an emergency should be declared, set up the Office of Price Administration and Civilian Supply. Its Administrator has been hampered, however, by uncertainty as to his duties. Finally, finding himself ineffective, he asked for defining legislation. This is embodied in a bill now before the Congress.

It appears that, if the situation is to be met in any adequate way, certain measures will need to be taken by the Insular Government. What those may be, in view of impending legislation, is not in every respect clear. But it is clear that certain things will have to be done in any case. Because of the uncertainties of Federal control, as well as because of Puerto Rico's situation, it would seem best to set up an organization which can meet the crisis in alternate ways and with degrees of intensity suited to developments which cannot be predicted.

81

It is, therefore, recommended that the Governor be given certain powers which may be delegated to an Administrator of Civilian Supply. These powers might not have to be used; or only part of them might be required. It would be foolish to bring into being an organization larger than the emergency should demand. On the other hand, it would be equally foolish not to be equipped with suitable instruments to meet any situation which might arise. It seems best, therefore, to grant the Executive a certain leeway in these matters. Certain findings, made publicly, ought to bring into action processes envisaged in advance and anticipated by the Legislature.

The situation is not dissimilar to that which existed in 1917 and was met by Joint Resolution 10, of 12 April 1917. In this Act the Legislature set up the Insular Food Commission with power to fix prices, enter into the distribution of produce when necessary and generally to control profiteering or restriction of supplies. The powers given then appear to have been adequate and experience with their use satisfactory. (See *Report* by the Food Commission, 1917). In this Act there were virtually no legislative standards to guide the execution of the mission. It would seem that some might properly be imposed.

Study of this earlier legislation and consideration of the prospects for inflation during the coming months, and perhaps years, ought to guide the Legislature to a measure which will set up an agency firm but flexible; economical but adequate.

It is further recommended that the need for transferring purchasing power from the present to the future be met by adjusting Insular income, excess profits and estate taxes to the new levels established in the Federal Revenue Act of 1941, making these increases proportionate to the relationship heretofore existing and widening the base on which the taxes are established.

Such tax increases will produce more revenue than will be needed or ought to be expended at this time by the Insular Government. The funds so secured will, however, be available to assist in the inevitable postwar shift from defense to civilian production. If I thought it would be acceptable, I should recommend even heavier taxes and perhaps the establishment of an unemployment fund. It is too early to expect actual unemployment insurance, though it is to be hoped that we may attain it sometime soon. Indeed, it is the subject of special study now by a commission which will report to the regular session of the Legislature. Something approaching the same effect could be got now by taxes shared by workers and employers. This would also have the desirable result of transferring purchasing power into the future. It has been the general opinion of others, however, that such a tax at this time would be inexpedient. It is argued that workers in Puerto Rico have too low a level of wages anyway, and that any tax on them would be unwarranted. My own fear is that an increase in prices will constitute such a tax in any case, if some purchasing power is not withdrawn from the market; and that this tax will go to speculators rather than be saved by the government for future use. If control measures are completely successful, this will not happen; and in any case, much of the price rise will occur outside Puerto Rico. I have, therefore, given way on that point. But I feel that these arguments do not apply to such purchasing power as may be withdrawn through higher income taxes. And they will help to build up a certain reserve to be used for post-emergency public works.

The Federal Government has already begun the building up of a ''shelf of projects'', to be available when needed. If former practice were followed, a certain local contribution would be expected. The former experience was that available funds were used in localities where matching was readiest. By such management as is here suggested, matching funds would be available in Puerto Rican or Federal securities and so might be multiplied by whatever contribution to local projects the Federal Government should decide to make.

It is suggested, however, out of former experience, that 10 per cent should be set aside at once for the acquisition of land and for planning. Public works usually require land which is not already publicly owned. The processes of surveying, taking title and gaining possession are often protracted. Many a project in recent years has been lost because the land on which to operate was not immediately available. Communities which are most forehanded in this respect are the best served. If it is not uncommon for the acquisition of land to require a year or more, the site and detail planning often require at least another year so that even with funds available construction may not begin at all for two years or more. Meantime unemployment may grow worse and privation intensify. Something like this happened in the last depression.

It is out of a desire to avoid these delays and difficulties that Federal and local officials are now being asked to decide definitely on at least a minimum number of projects, to acquire all necessary land for them, and to carry forward their planning to the point where they can begin at once when the need for employment arises. Those given employment on roads, schools, hospitals, sewers, playgrounds, and other works, will buy from those who perform other productive services, the whole forming that economic chain which, when broken, prostrates the whole community.

Two subsidiary measures are also necessary and ought to be passed at once: provision for increased personnel to manage tax collections, a suggested schedule of which will be presented; and provision for a central statistical service in the Office of the Governor. For this latter purpose a much simpler bill is needed than Senate 179, passed at the last session but vetoed by the Governor.

It is desired at this time to point out briefly the relation of all the foregoing to the Puerto Rican Planning Commission which will be proposed to the regular session later in the year and to the action of the National Resources Planning Board in establishing here a Regional Office.

Assuming that legislation approving a Planning Commission is passed in somewhat the same form as has been followed in several hundred other communities, that Commission will be charged with the duties of establishing a Master Plan, having custody of the Official Map, and controlling the formulation of a Capital Budget for one year and a Program for several years beyond that.

The Master Plan will show projects in their relative importance, properly located, and the Capital Budget and Program will show the source and method of financing. If we now provide for a fund which can be used for such projects, supplementing Federal funds which flow much more readily to localities whose planning is trustworthy, we shall not only be in a position to go to work promptly, but shall be assured that the work will be done where it will count most.

It is perhaps necessary to say, in connection with the 10

per cent to be set aside for land and planning, that no more than one per cent of that will need to go to the Planning Commission. Its work will not usually include detail, but only the overhead or central planning. The detail planning for actual ocnstruction will remain as before in the executive departments.

In constructing the Master Plans in the first instance, which is a long, tedious and extremely expert task, it is fortunate that the regional office of the National Resources Planning Board will be available for assistance with its relations to the home office in Washington and the various experts on its staff. It is also fortunate that the Public Works Reserve under the Federal Works Agency will be at work collecting and classifying for Federal aid the various projects here which may be eligible.

The whole: the funds in reserve for unemployment and various ways of planning ought to bring us to the next crisis of unemployment far better prepared than ever has been true in the past. And if the tax measure assists to keep down the cost of living in the present, so much more will have been gained.

II

The obtaining of a safe and adequate supply of water and completely sanitary disposal of sewerage is a problem which torments any rapidly growing city. This is because the funds for expansion increase less rapidly than the demand. Funds for expansion are usually obtained through assessment and there is always determined opposition to increases in assessment or the tax rate which are in proportion to the growth of population and values. This comes oftenest, perhaps, from speculative real estate developers who hope that others can be made to bear the burden; but, also, sometimes from home owners themselves who do not realize the connection between taxes and service or who have reason to believe that it is not as direct as it ought to be.

It is a matter of general knowledge that San Juan, particularly, but other municipalities as well, has suffered and is suffering in these respects to a degree which constitutes an emergency. Not only is there an immense amount of defense activity at stake, but also there is the intensified danger that we are within the tropics and subject to certain peculiar dangers. It would not be profitable to assess the blame for deficiency. It is much more helpful to find a way to provide service.

To do this it is necessary in the first place to entrust expansion, maintenance, and service work to an organization which beyond any doubt enjoys the confidence of investors and of the public. For the immediate purpose the word investor may be thought of as referring to certain Federal agencies. For only through them can funds be had at the moment or priorities be granted for construction.

With this in mind I have explored in Washington the possibilities in a preliminary way and have learned that only by a complete transfer of responsibility can the way be opened to recognition of the problem as one affecting defense and worthy of respect as one to be solved with defense funds. The conclusion is that if San Juan and other areas desire in the immediate future to see the situation corrected, a wholly new solution has to be found. I think it only fair to warn everyone concerned, also, that, in my judgment, no compromise will have the desired effect. There is no doubt among lending agencies as to the emergency or even of its connection with national defense. But there is doubt as to whether funds granted or loaned will be well administered. On this point they will demand to be fully satisfied.

I have concluded in view of the emergency and of the attitude which I discovered to exist that I ought to recommend to the Legislature the assumption of these services by the most logical agency: the new Water Resources Authority which has not only, under its old name, demonstrated efficiency in force-account construction, in the handling of water and in service relations with consumers, but which, under its new one, enjoys such a reputation with investors and particularly with Federal agencies that it would have a real chance of obtaining defense grants at once and loan funds in the future.

To use this ready resort would enable us to escape from the dilemma of needs which grow more rapidly than resources. Defense funds are given without local matching, in recognition of need. If these could be obtained in any considerable amount, local resources could be used to strenghten the situation still more in the future. And such a start will have been made that the vicious circle will be broken. I consider it so desirable to achieve this that I have no hesitation in recommending modification in this instance of municipal responsibility. In a case like the present, which has many points of likeness with electric power generation and distribution, in which action has been taken, changes ought to be made before the situation degenerates even further.

It is also to be noted that a number of the water systems of Puerto Rico already extend over more than one municipality, sometimes, as in the case of the capital, over several. The principle of municipal autonomy has already become greatly modified. No great change is involved in carrying the consolidation further for such purposes as this. Management has progressed in recent years so that the controls necessary to a unit of the size which would include the whole of our island are readily available. Indeed, they are already being used for the purpose of making and distributing electric power.

To make the organization which devised and which operates the one responsible also for the other will involve certain economies which are worth noting. How great these will be cannot be estimated with any accuracy, but the savings will certainly be substantial.

III

It is recommended that the Special Session establish in close cooperation with the College of Agriculture and Mechanic Arts and the Agricultural Experiment Station of the Federal Government at Mayagüez, an Institute of Tropical Agriculture; for this purpose it is recommended that there be appropriated immediately one hundred thousand dollars to make a beginning and that it be declared to be the intention of the Legislature to appropriate forty thousand dollars per year for the ten years succeeding.

To effectuate the policy, it is recommended that there be set up a Board of Trustees of nine members; five of whom shall first be appointed by the Governor for terms of 2, 4, 6, 8, and 10 years and who shall thereafter be elected by a majority of the Board; and four of whom shall be as follows: one selected by the Insular Commissioner of Agriculture, one by the Federal Secretary of Agriculture, one by the Director of the Pan American Union, and one by the Chancellor of the University of Puerto Rico.

When constituted, this Board is recommended to have the power of selecting a Director, who may be the Director of the Federal station.

It is recommended that the policy of this Institute be announced as that of fundamental as well as applied research, and that its activities be oriented to the peculiar effects of tropic sun, of soils within these latitudes of the Western Hemisphere and of the air currents and pressures which distinguish the Caribbean. To achieve the desired results, it is recommended that a small company of scientists and advanced students be entertained at the Institute, sometimes without pay other than subsistence and living quarters. It may be found feasible to award degrees, but this ought not to be the first emphasis. The establishment of this Institute in a formal way does no more than to recognize what has been taking place for a long time. Scientists and students have found the Experimental Station at Mayagüez a fascinating resort. But many difficulties of a practical sort intervene when their visits are prolonged enough to be useful. It is believed that the setting up of an institute, whose center will be merely a Guest Hause and Guest Laboratory, may be the beginning of a profitable venture into exploration. It is not impossible that it may attract support and funds from the many agencies which are just becoming interested in the tropics, in Latin America, and the new central importance of Puerto Rico.

In this connection Puerto Ricans do not need to be reminded that such an Institute has long been projected here; and that plans for it have on more than one occasion been far advanced. For one reason or another, these reasons always being fortuitous, and having nothing to do with the merits of the project, plans have never actually borne fruit. It will be recalled, for instance, that in 1928 a committee of the National Research Council visited the Island and recommended the establishment of a Graduate School of Tropical Agriculture. And that in 1932 a project was almost consummated for a School or Institute, with Cornell University sharing responsibility with the University of Puerto Rico in its conduct. The plan then, however, depended upon the gift by an individual of a large sum of money and when that gift did not materialize, the project was abandoned. That lack; I think, need not deter us under present circumstances. An institution with the support of the Puerto Rican government and linked with its University will not fail. Funds for a building program and for endowment would be welcome. But it may be that such funds would be attracted to an actually going institution.

In this same connection, it is further recommended that the Legislature authorize by a special appropriation a School of Public Administration. In my inaugural address I pointed out the possibilities of bettering the public service and said that the chief source of this improvement lay in the University. The University could, however, be better organized to supply both men and procedures. It has a School of Law and a School of Business Administration; but both these supply training mostly for private employment. It is true that an accountant, even though trained for business, may be useful, for instance, in the Treasury; but this is an incidental, almost accidental, concurrence. It is not expected or required. There is a great field of public administration which has opened more and more to young talent in the last few decades. With the expansion of the public service during the depression years and now in the crisis of national defense, it has been vastly expanded. And it has been made more attractive in the career sense by the outlawing everywhere of the old-fashioned political preferment. That will take place in Puerto Rico, too. But it is the opening up to our young men and women of careers not only in the Insular service but in the Federal service as well, that I have in mind.

The respect with which Civil Service examiners and selection officers of other sorts regard candidates coupled with formal training in administration is notable. Some of that respect ought to be diverted to Puerto Rican youths. The curriculum of such a school includes Personnel Management, Budgeting Practice, Paper Work Processes, Administrative Controls, Fiscal Theories, Public Law, Social Philosophy, Industrial and Commercial Effects of Government Policy, Political and Economic Geography, the Theory and Practice of Public Accounting, etc., etc.—a range of subjects either not treated at all or regarded from a wholly different point of view in the curriculum of a School of Law or of Business.

My suggestion for this purpose would be that the Legislature appropriate, outside other University funds, $5,000 for

the half year beginning with the second semester of this year
for the purpose of putting some competent person to work
at the organization of such a school and that beginning with
the first semester of the next year $25,000 be provided which
would grow to $75,000 annually by the third year.

I also suggest that the School of Public Administration
and the Law School should be provided with a joint building
and library. Such a building could not be built at once, but
planning for it, which would require at least a year, could
be begun at once. Including land, such an institution ought
to cost about $250,000 which, in view of the long-run ad-
vantages can well be afforded.

IV

The Act establishing the Minimum Wage Board recently
approved by the Legislature has been found to contain certain defects which would prevent the functioning of the
Board on a sound basis if they were not corrected before the
Board is organized and begins to function. This is a very
important piece of legislation and we should move cautiously
to insure the proper operation of the Act and of the agency
created by it.

The Act makes it mandatory for the Governor to request
candidates for membership in the Board from employers and
from industrial, agricultural and commercial associations, as
well as from the workers and labor organizations of the
Island.

This may cause complaint from associations or individual
employers or workers who were not requested to submit
candidates for the Board. The wording of the Act should
be changed so as to give to any industrial, commercial or agricultural organization, or to any individual employer and to
labor organizations, unions and individual workers the right
to nominate candidates for membership on the Board. From
the persons thus nominated the Governor would select those
who in his judgment are best qualified to discharge the duties
of said office.

The appropriation of funds for the Minimum Wage Board
has been made for specified positions in the general budget
of expenses for the fiscal year 1941–42. However, certain
key positions which are indispensable to the proper function-

ing of the Board, such as economists, statisticians, account ants, etc., have not been provided for. The Board will have to make a complete study of each industry before the minimum wages, hours of work and conditions of employment for said industry may be established. This has to be done in an unbiased, scientific manner for which highly trained and specialized personnel will have to be engaged. At salaries fixed in the present Budget Act it would be impossible to obtain the services of competent persons for this type of work. It is recommended therefore that a lump sum of $30,000 be appropriated for the Board for the remainder of the present fiscal year, the budgetary distribution of such funds to be made by the Chairman of the Board with the approval of the Governor of Puerto Rico.

The Act as now in effect provides that the Board as a whole shall have authority to appoint its personnel. This is deemed very unsatisfactory. It is a sound administrative principle that the person who is responsible for the administration of an office shall have the authority to select the persons who are to work under him and for whose acts he must answer. This general principle has special bearing in the case of the Minimum Wage Board which is composed of members representing different points of view and in which many controversial matters will have to be settled. If the Chairman, who is the only full-time member of the Board and its executive officer, has to share his authority for the selection of personnel with the other eight members of the Board, he cannot be made responsible for the proper and efficient functioning of the agency.

As the Act is now worded each member has the right to nominate candidates for positions on the Board. The administration and enforcement of the Act should be divorced from the functions of the Board and left in the hands of its executive officer. The public interests will be best served if the Chairman of the Board is made solely responsible for all executive and administrative matters including the selection of personnel.

REXFORD G. TUGWELL,
Governor.

LA FORTALEZA, *October 28, 1941.*

Puerto Rico's hunger was continuously in the Governor's mind. The children suffered most and he knew it.

MEMBERS OF THE LEGISLATURE:

I am informed that an increase of $100,000 in the spon-
sors contribution to the school lunch project will result in the
expenditure of approximately $500,000 for this work.

The benefits from this project are so numerous that there
can hardly be any objection to such an enlargement. The
gains to child health are so basic and so real that I have no
hesitation in recommending that the appropriation be made
at this time.

Respecfully yours,

R. G. TUGWELL,
Governor.

LA FORTALEZA, *November 6, 1941.*

In keeping with the Governor's recommendation, the Legislature in the Special Session created a commission to attempt, insofar as it lay within the power of the Insular Government, to control the import, distribution and price of Puerto Rico's living necessities. This agency was set up on November 17, three weeks before Pearl Harbor. It was not as efficient as the Governor had hoped, because it diffused its administrative power in the hands of several commissioners rather than centralizing it in one administrator as the Governor had asked.

This session of the Legislature increased the Insular income tax. After the change it more closely approximated the existing Federal tax. It authorized a reorganization of the Treasury Department. It created the island's first office of centralized statistics. It provided means by which the island's ancient aqueducts could be taken over and improved by the Water Resources Authority for the protection of the health of the people. It established an Institute of Tropical Agriculture and a School of Public Affairs, agencies the Governor hoped would enhance Puerto Rico as a link between northern technical skill and southern technical needs.

From the beginning, the Coalition, led by Resident Commissioner (non-voting Congressman) Bolívar Pagán, accused the Governor of being the political tool of the Popular-Liberal majority of the Legislature. The groundlessness of this charge was clearly evidenced in Mr. Tugwell's veto of a coffee subsidy bill.

The Governor's awareness of the war problem, and the vigor of his opposition to needless spending in relation to it, are stated directly in this message, one month before Pearl Harbor.

VETO MESSAGE

When, on 5 November 1941, I sent a call to the special session of the legislature asking consideration for the problems of the coffee industry, I explained that numerous conferences had not brought about agreement as to what ought to be done. I thought, therefore, that the Legislature ought to take some measure of an emergency nature, meanwhile setting up a commission for the formulation of a permanent policy. I made the condition that enough revenue be provided through the income tax to meet any outlays involved.

The condition was not complied with. The increased yield of the income tax will not nearly equal the $750,000 appropriated in this bill for subsidies.

Aside from this, however, the bill merits disapproval for other reasons. As I have studied it I have had a deepening conviction that it would not accomplish the purposes for which it was intended. These were stated: "to increase the purchasing power of coffee growers, to better the wages of workers who grow and process this product, to encourage commerce, to benefit the consuming public, and to preserve the forests in the coffee zones of Puerto Rico and the supply of water resources of Puerto Rico."

What it would certainly do, in my judgment, is to increase enormously the profits of speculators and exporters. Some gains might be made by growers, but not more probably than they would get under present circumstances and with legislation now in force if that were properly implemented.

After the statement of purposes, the interests of workers and all the other admirable intentions were apparently forgot, for no conditions whatever are attached to the payment of the subsidy. As a matter of fact, it would go directly to "every natural or artificial person who exports coffee." No relief is offered, in my judgment, to Puerto Rican consumers in the section providing for home consumption and no scheme is included by which they might be encouraged to consume more of the product grown on this Island. If the subsidy had the effect of expanding home consumption, the burden on taxpayers might be more justifiable. Nor is there any limitation whatever on traders' profits. The subsidy is to be based on a calculation which "allows a net liquidation for the coffee growers of Puerto Rico of not less than 15 cents"; but it is to be paid to exporters, not to growers, and there is no means of determining these relationships in such ways as would protect the growers in the slightest degree.

Beyond these considerations the law does not even make a gesture toward those permanent conservation measures indicated in the statement of purpose. Nor does it recognize in any way the need for protection of growers against the hazards of hurricane. Fortunately a supplementary act was passed which provides for study of these problems and the formulation of a permanent scheme. The Legislature when it meets again a few months from now will be in a position to consider whether the purposes enumerated in this bill can not in some way be met. It is to be hoped also that if new legislation is formulated the administrative provisions of this bill will not be used as precedent. Those clauses alone would justify disapproval.

They provide for a Board of seven members, two of whom are ex-officio, three of whom are dictated by exporters and the Farmers' Association, and one of whom represents coffee cooperatives organizations. There is one to represent consumers and this member alone is to be nominated freely by the Governor. This is an undisguised attempt to pack an administrative board with representatives of private interests and has to be energically rejected. If "the executive" is to be in any sense responsible for the carrying out of laws he ought not to be limited in this way, and particularly by delegating his duties without his consent to those who have an interest in their use.

It must not be supposed that my disapproval of this bill indicates a lack of sympathy on my part or on the part of other administrative officers with the difficulties of coffee farmers. The Legislature has shown its sympathy by passing this bill. If I disapprove it that is because I believe that more relief can be provided for the farmer in another way. If the legislature had not authorized three-quarters of a million dollars in subsidies in this bill, the Treasurer, the Commissioner of Agriculture, the Auditor and I, myself, might have been more reluctant to provide the funds necessary to the operations of the Stabilizing Corporation now in existence. The reason for this former reluctance was that no losses were apparently antcipated or provided for in the legislation; and if they were incurred, they might well have been charged to bad judgment among administrative officials.

None of them felt that operations could be carried out without losses if the first care was to bring relief to the farmer. But if the legislative intention is not against, but rather for, subsidy to the industry then the Corporation now in existence is a better vehicle for operations than the Board provided for in the new act. If its losses are clearly to be regarded as a function of its relief efforts then there is less objection to assuming responsibility for their almost certain occurrence. Since the Corporation does not simply give out funds but tries to see that returns come to growers through improving the export market and stabilizing the domestic the burden on the taxpayer is certain to be far less than it might be under the new bill. A fair price is better than a subsidy. The Corporation will work for fair prices and keep the subsidies within the closest possible limits.

The Corporation is, therefore, being provided immediately the funds necessary for its operations. All administrative officials are cooperating so that no red tape may interfere. Farmers will find, I am assured by officials of the Corporation and by the Auditor, that they can bring their coffee to specified places and receive payment simply and directly. The distinction between the export and the domestic quotas will begin after this transaction and will not interfere with payment.

Everything that can be done will be done to insure the orderly marketing and storage of the large crop now being harvested. The Corporation officials are experienced and sympathetic. I hope they may have the cooperation of all genuine members of the coffee growing fraternity.

When it is seen what relief can be brought to farmers by this method, and how costly it is, the legislative commission will have actual data for its further consideration of a policy for the industry.

This year's operation cannot be more costly than the revenue provided in the additions to the income tax. It thus meets a condition which seems to me imperative. It has been said that the Treasury is able to meet the $750,000 bill for subsidy provided in the alternate measure. As to that, such extra revenue as is now available ought to be used, in all

103

common sense, for the refinancing of the debt. Great savings can now be made in interest payments if this is competently done. The Treasurer intends to do it. But he must have funds to carry out such an operation. There is also the added necessity of restoring to the emergency fund borrowings in leaner years. There will come disaster; there always has come disaster. Among those who will suffer most and have the heaviest claims for relief will be coffee farmers. I should like to keep the emergency fund intact for their sake if for that of no other group.

These are only two of numerous weighty reasons for not incurring greater current obligations than are necessary to efficient and enlightened administration. We ought to spend what is necessary in planning for the future and for taking every precaution against the vast risks of our time. But we ought also to keep in the forefront of our consideration the need which will surely come for credit when some one of those risks is no longer avoidable and an emergency occurs.

To reduce the debt; to reduce the carrying charge of the debt outstanding; to make credit good and so to have a ready recource in the margin of borrowing capacity: this is the policy to which I believe the Puerto Rican government ought to devote itself at this moment.

There will come a time for spending, and spending freely. This is the time to rearrange, to forego, to perfect organization, and to plan. If I insist on provision of new revenue for any new expenditure, this is the reason. I believe it will commend itself to thoughtful citizens.

The Coalition soon became convinced that its partisan attacks on the Governor on the grounds of patronage would not succeed in discrediting him in the eyes of President Roosevelt. Tactics were, therefore, changed. The new strategy was to paint the Governor as a "Quisling," dangerously dividing the island in time of war, giving the States the mistaken impression of uncertain loyalty. Actually, Mr. Tugwell was using every opportunity to show the mainland the island's faith and courage.

RADIOGRAM SENT TO THE DIVISION OF TERRITORIES AND ISLAND POSSESSIONS, INTERIOR DEPARTMENT, WASHINGTON, ON NOVEMBER 6, 1941, FOR INCLUSION IN A TERRITORIES BROADCAST.

It is not surprising that the reaction of Puerto Rico to the cause of Democracy, Humanity and Freedom, at this very crucial moment of historical development has been prompt, warm and enthusiastic. Puerto Ricans could not have failed their long tradition of devoted faith in the good causes for which mankind has struggled and suffered and died throughout the centuries.

At the present crisis when two irreconciliable philosophies of living are engaged in a fight to the death, the trend of the island has been unanimous. Not a single act of sabotage has been registered here. Not one group of propagandists against the policies of our Nation is in existence. No organ of public opinion, from the largest to the humblest, has declined to express its hearty agreement with our leaders in Washington, who point out to us the very real danger of the future and the inescapable necessity, if we are to overcome those dangers, of uniting for the task of resisting those powers whose leaders would destroy the human spirit.

Such a spirit is not new to our island. Its loyalty and its love of liberty and its capacity of resisting the thrusts of aggression has been demonstrated in epic sagas of the past as it is being materialized today through splendid cooperation and discipline.

As far back as the 16th century our community began to harden in the grim experiences of war and bloodshed. Unending wars were raging then between the Mother Country and England. Queen Elizabeth and King Phillip the II, two of the most powerful rulers of the existing world, struggled fiercely over the possession of Puerto Rico, then, as now, a coveted stronghold in the defense of the Americas. Proud warriors of the past, whose names graced history with their valiant feats and romantic adventures: Sir Francis Drake, Hawkins, the Duke of Cumberland, Admiral Abercromby, Harvey, met defeat and disappointment at the shores of Puerto Rico where the proud forts of Spain defended by a scant garrison and by untrained islanders, still stand as reminders of those brave events.

In 1625 it was the brilliant Navy of the "Prince of Orange" the then ruler of the Netherlands, which was to experience a disastrous defeat at the hands of my distinguished predecessor, Governor De Haro, who broke the backbone of the Dutch invaders in cooperation with the Puerto Rican militia, on the peaceful meadows of "El Morro" where golf is now played.

In 1597 the Duke of Cumberland delivered a blow which, like the previous one, was unsuccessful. Finally in 1797 England sent to the conquest of Puerto Rico one of its ablest naval leaders, Admiral Abercromby, who had won glory and renown at the battle of the Nile, fighting, side by side, with Admiral Nelson. With him was the famous Harvey. The battle, fought at the walls of San Gerónimo fortress, was carried on the one side by a great fleet of English units, and on the other by another of my illustrious predecessors, Captain General De Castro, who at the head of 4,000 Puerto Rican militiamen, inflicted a crushing defeat upon the invaders.

After the treaty of Paris, which marked the end of hostilities between Spain and the United States in 1898, Puerto Rico had one more opportunity to test its unflinching loyalty. That was in the first World War when over 20,000 Puerto Ricans were mobilized to defend the "Stars and Stripes" and when 55 members of our community gave their lives in Argonne and Chauteau-Thierry for the cause.

It is thus, small wonder, that we are again ready and alert for whatever may come in the fight for the great cause of Humanity. I can assure you that all of Puerto Rico is ready to go as far as necessary, regardless of sacrifices and without concern for privation or suffering, in order that we may live to see the survival of the great institutions of liberty which inspire the very soul of our Nation.

TUGWELL,
Governor.

Although immersed in war work and heavily burdened with its new problems, the Governor could not limit his view to the horizon of the struggle. He looked beyond, toward the time when the bloodshed should cease. His reason for this was not the whim of a capricious dreamer, but the experience of the last armistice. He remembered its great hope. He regretted its great tragedy.

ARMISTICE DAY ADDRESS
SAN JUAN, NOVEMBER 11, 1941.

FELLOW CITIZENS:

There is no man of my generation who does not have
vivid recollections of that first armistice day which we are
celebrating here. Whether he was a member of the armed
forces or whether he served in some civilian way, his recollections are equally sharp. For all of us had been engaged
in what had seemed to us a crusade. And on that day our
hopes seemed to have been fulfilled. The struggle had been
defined as one to make the world safe for democracy. This
meant that free men might work out their ways of living in
peace, and that the resort to force was forever outlawed. A
new era had come, in which vast accomplishments would be
made, the world transformed—or so we thought. It was for
this that millions had died and millions more had been
maimed, that young men had given their careers, that mothers
had given their sons.

The Day of Armistice was a kind of climax. The years
of steady sacrifice were over, the long tensions were relaxed.
We might now go back to the old enterprises of peace, building homes, raising crops, making goods, perfecting social organization. No one thought the future was a workless one
or one in which differences would not appear. It did seem,
however, that work might be done, differences settled without some savage running amok with deadly weapons. There
never had been a time when that was true, though it had
sometimes seemed so: the Victorian days, the era which came
after our Civil War. It had seemed then, briefly, as though
the institutions of peace were permanent. It had not been
all it seemed. Not only were the seeds of destruction sown
by the Imperialists and by the captains of business; but
also the organization of peace was delayed and neglected.
So that when a nodule of ruthlessness appeared there was
no way to contain and suppress it. It was even encouraged
by those among ourselves who were more devoted to private
gain than to the common good.

But all that was past now. The nucleus of force had expanded and had been lanced. We could breathe again. But
more than that our struggle had been enriched and defined

by a leader who now would see, as the peace was shaped, that the institutions of peace were strong and vigilant. Force had been outlawed and would never rise again. Our sons would never have to drop their work, leave their wives, and submit to the disciplines of war.

All this was in the minds of men at eleven o'clock on the morning of November 11th in 1918. On that morning I was in Paris as the guns began to thunder along the outer ruin of fortifications a salute to the new Peace. The steady rhythm jarred the building in which I worked as it had been jarred many times before by shells or aerial bombs. This, I thought to myself, will be the last reverberations of that sound. For I, like others, had visions of artillery sunk in the sea or melted to make some article of daily use.

It was such a heavy morning as is characteristic of the Ile de France in November. A kind of ghostly sun behind the Seine valley's mists modified but little the gloom and chill of the lightless night we had just come through. Yet no sun ever seemed so full of glowing promise, I thought, as I looked out of my window onto the *Place Theatre Francais* where, a month before, a great bomb pit had been. Now the fountain would flow again, children would play in the Place, old men sit in the sun, and Parisian crowds stream into and out of the *Theatre*

I recall what happened then: I walked down into the *Place* and walked up the *Avenue de L'Opera*. The *Avenue* was all but deserted at that moment, as, I thought, it will never be again. But plodding down it, close to the curb, an old woman came. She was pushing a great cart heaped with turnips and in the topmost a little flag of France was stuck. As she came opposite, I saw that she was in widow's weeds and that her face streamed with tears. The glory of victory and passionate hope, the sacrifice and the sorrow—all were there. And although I went on to see and experience many other things on that day, no other has stayed so clearly in my memory as that old woman of France, drowned in brave tears, yet with the flag flying on her cargo of turnips.

That all the sacrifice should have been in vain, all the hopes disappointed, is the tragedy of our time. We had the energy to win the war but not the wisdom to organize the peace.

Now we are in the midst of another effort to suppress an unlimited appeal to force which is again loose in the world. Some time soon—we may hope—there will come another Day of Armistice. We shall have another chance to be generous, patient and wise. It is my prayer now that we may use it to achieve those purposes which escaped us before. And that, this time, we may really sterilize the sources of violence on this earth.

The war in the Pacific was two months and three days old when the Puerto Rican Legislature opened the first regular session of Mr. Tugwell's administration. There had been exciting days on the island just after Pearl Harbor, and there had been much confusion. Now things were settling down again and not many people could see a very clear danger in the future.

The Governor, who had talked before about the fact that the island's basic foods were imported, talked now about the necessity of accumulating food stock-piles. He expected prompt help from Congress. He could not know that there his work was to be sabotaged by the island's own representative, the Resident Commissioner Bolívar Pagán.

Ignorant of Pagán's intention, confident the people would not go hungry, the Governor urged the Legislature not to permit the war to be used by selfish interests to halt social progress which was "a generation overdue".

MESSAGE TO THE FIFTEENTH LEGISLATURE
AT ITS SECOND REGULAR SESSION.

INTRODUCTION

No legislature in the history of Puerto Rico has had to meet in circumstances more difficult than those of the present. You represent a people living in an armed outpost of the United States. As such it might at any time be attacked— not, of course, in force, so long as the fleet holds the Atlantic and a hostile African shore lies at the back of any enemy. The worst that might happen at present is a sporadic attack from sea or air. But even that might cost lives and cause damage.

It is a tragic circumstance that the labors of this Legislature should have to be carried on under the shadow of war. The fact of conflict is an overwhelming one. It is difficult to consider other actions than those which have to do with the defeat of the enemy or defense against his encroachments. Yet I have to tell you that it must be done. The condition of our people reflects years of injustice and neglect. Whether we have war or peace we must attempt to set going movements which in time will lift people out of slums and will exorcise hunger. They are entitled to shelter, to food— and to more than that. But the margin above misery they will create for themselves, if we establish the chance.

Our people cannot be set upon this way of progress unless government itself is improved. It is not now an instrument well shaped for a war on poverty and disease. But to improve government is a long task at which we shall be working for years; and meanwhile we must go ahead. It would be better, far better, if you, as legislators, were free from the dangers which beset us and could deliberate at leisure and in peace. It would be better, far better, if the beginnings of social justice had been established in former years. But we must accept conditions as they are since they are beyond our control. We must proceed as best we can.

Going ahead with such a program does not mean that measures for defense are to be neglected. On the contrary, everything possible must be done to insure the safety of the civil population while our army and navy attend professionally to offense. In the weeks while you are meeting, there will be settled a number of crucial questions involving the division of expenditure for civil defense between the Federal and Insular governments. These will be brought as rapidly as possible to issue and transmitted for your consideration. Of these matters, and others having to do with the program of action, I have made a more extended memorandum which I shall send for your consideration. I confine myself on this occasion to greeting you and wishing you well on your deliberations.

Beyond this greeting I think it not inappropriate to say to you that in my heart these days there is a swelling thankfulness: I have been permitted to live for more than fifty years of my own life in a free land. No matter what happens, that cannot be taken from me. And I conceive that, in spite of territorial status which satisfies no one, and in spite of misunderstandings and differences, some of them considerable, you as Puerto Ricans share my gratitude. For you have had the same citizenship for many years. And the benefits of the Bill of Rights—and of all those liberties we associate with the Bill of Rights—have been yours no less than mine.

As civilians we feel, all of us, these days a deep dissatisfaction that we cannot be in uniform and so show where we stand and what we are willing to undergo for the preservation of those freedoms we have so long and thoughtlessly enjoyed. For when we are made to think of it, we are determined that they shall not be destroyed. Even though the better part of our own lives are past, and for us personally much of their value is over, we want them for our sons and daughters. We realize all at once that this is worth all the rest of life. Many of those who have gone before have said again and again that death itself is a small price to pay for freedom. And we had rather fallen into the way of thinking that words like these and the deeds which followed them were more than half bombastic. We understand, now when there is actual challenge, that the words which defined our priviledges were genuine and that the deeds which followed were actually heroic. We, too, may have to use such words in all seriousness and stand for them until we die. They ring like new-minted coins now on the granite of minds which never before were wholly clear.

118

The months and years of tension have straightened thought. To us, too, life seems a little thing beside those mighty principles we had always regarded as common to us all, not to be thought about particularly, just to be taken for granted. And we are resolved, not as men who have been ordered to a duty, but as sober citizens who have pondered these matters in solitary thought, that we too are quite ready to die that our children may be free.

You and I and all of us have been critical of the institutions we now defend. Each of us has felt in his own way that he knew how they could be improved. This was the saving self-repairing element in democracy. This made it, in the long run, superior to any alternative. It is a simple proposition that encouragement of criticism and readiness to change make possible a permanent society; and that none is possible without them. Yet its truth has the power to penetrate the pretensious shell of personal infallibility everywhere. Sooner or later dictators make mistakes on a scale so grand that their empires disintegrate and disappear. No democracy can make a mistake like that. It can be slow in decision while all the people absorb facts and conclude their policy. It can be inefficient because it suspects the expert. But the running comment of many minds prevents the building up of such vast vulnerable edifices of falsity as totalitarianism makes conceivable. And that is why, when we begin to win, we shall win everywhere and quickly; because our power will grow and that of our enemies will crumble.

Our system has its faults. Our care for a free press and free assembly opens us to abuses which sometimes seem intolerable, almost treasonable. Our slowness to achieve substantial unanimity on great questions sometimes brings us to our crises unprepared so that long beyond their climaxes we fumble for the right kind of organization. And time, in this technological age, has been our enemy.

Perhaps the greatest fault of our system, and the one which sometimes has seemed the cause of its future destruction, is its tolerance of injustice. In our desire for personal freedom, it has often been forgot that freedom to exploit, to push others down, to refuse them opportunity, is not one of the guarantees for which our forefathers risked their lives. The maintenance of equal chance for equal ability, the establishment of minimums of living and health, these are necessary to any real freedom at all. To argue that men must be free to underpay their workers, for instance, is like the specious argument for freedom of speech in order to destroy it. Those are not the freedoms we fight for. They are not freedoms at all. They are franchises for destruction which we must eliminate from society before we can make any progress. It is just here, as legislators, that you have a duty. And not only in spite of war, but all the more because of war. If it is totalitarianism we are fighting, we have to fight it with legislative bills and administrative effort just as much as with planes and tanks.

Remember that you do your work behind a rampart of heroic sacrifice. What soldiers and sailors are doing for a better world you can surely have the civilian courage to share. Take the strokes of your enemies as others are taking the strokes of other enemies. Be worthy of your fighting comrades. Gain something of social justice and you will have served in the same campaign.

I am moved to acknowledge here that vast debt of gratitude we owe to multitudes of the living and dead in Russia, in China, in Britain, in those other tropical islands opposite us on this globe—the Dutch Indies—and even in the occupied nations. They have given us what we had to have—time: time to plan machines with which to build other machines. And since ours are later, they are likely to be better. Those people wanted what we too wanted. They hated what we hated. We have the duty now to finish what, at so great a sacrifice, they began. And if we win, we owe their children, along with ours, the better world for which they fought and, if need be, died.

It is an atmosphere of high enterprise, of vast risks, of a new world being born, that this Legislature meets. Let us be worthy of our time; do nothing out of malice; do everything for the less fortunate; regard no privilege as sacred; forget self; work to make Puerto Rico a worthy part of that world which the soldiers of freedom are creating.

1. CIVIL DEFENSE

Since the United States was attacked by Japan on December 7, the Government of Puerto Rico has been faced with the double task of preparing against danger, and preventing, while preparations were going on, the rise of hysteria which, in an emergency, might cause more harm than the event itself. It was necessary to organize a Civil Defense which should maintain discipline during alerts and be ready to preserve order and give aid if there should actually be need.

Short of creating a vast bureaucracy which would make and impose regulations, the only method to take was that of voluntary organization and service. This is admittedly a slower and more inefficient way. But it has the advantage of enlisting the cooperation of all earnest and patriotic citizens and of substituting a kind of self-discipline for arbitrary regulation. At any rate, this was the way chosen and the exigencies of the conflict have given us time to follow it. I had to judge against the advice of many who saw the situation differently that time would be given. Many would at once have imposed martial law, called the Legislature in session, closed all the schools and so on. But none of these was done.

This system can be said to have worked reasonably well everywhere but in the city of San Juan, where after weeks in which little progress toward organization was discernible, I relieved the local committee and appointed an administrator. This change, together with arrangements for closer technical advice by military experts, has put us on the way to satisfactory accomplishment.

By holding steady and working hard we have come this far, at least, without resort to measures which violate the individual's legitimate choices of what he shall or shall not do. Citizens, in hundreds and thousands, have joined in learning fire-prevention measures, in practicing the arts of first aid to the injured, of warden service and the like. And they have learned to respect regulations for protection which they recognize as reasonable. Only after considerable experience, I ventured to suggest a common ordinance for the municipalities which was worked out in the office of the Attorney General. Most of them adopted it and there are now beginning to be penalties for violation of the rules.

In the confusion of the first days of war, it was impossible to determine how much of the expense of Civil Defense would be borne by the Federal Government and how much would fall on the Insular Government; but it was also impossible to wait. I, therefore, solicited, and was freely granted, by the Emergency Fund Committee, $150,000 at first, and later an additional $150,000 to go 'on with. About half of this was used in ordering immediately quantities of medical supplies and establishing a blood bank; the larger part of the remainder was reserved for beginning the construction of air-raid shelters. This was as much as could be expended before the Legislature met and before some clear idea could be had of what the Federal Government would contribute. I shall send a later communication advising you of what help we may expect and what we shall need to do ourselves. And I shall not hesitate to ask for an amount adequate to carry us through the year.

It is a real pleasure to tell you that in all the difficult days we have come through, the Commandant of the 10th Naval District, Admiral John H. Hoover, and the Commander of the Puerto Rican Department, General James L. Collins, have given continuous cooperation. It has been our habit to meet frequently in my office for the exchange of complaints and information. I have sought to keep them in touch with the work of the Insular Government, to explain our limitations and to be of service when I could. They have put at my disposal their vast technical resources and their knowledge of the strategic situation. I think we have all of us appreciated the difficulties each of the others has had; and that the exchanges have helped us over a period which was full of pitfalls. On December 20 there was instituted a new Unity of Command in which the naval commander takes precedence in Puerto Rico. But this has not changed the admirable relationships which before existed. Admiral Hoover now becomes, in the period before us, responsible for all military activity. He has studied our problems and understands the Puerto Rican way of life. This Island is well guarded.

2. STATE GUARD

The Puerto Rico National Guard has now become part of the United States army for the duration of the war. To take its place Congress has authorized the organization of a State Guard. My choice of an officer to take charge of this work was General Luis Raúl Esteves who was in command of the old National Guard at Camp Tortuguero. There was some difficulty and some delay about securing his release but it was finally accomplished. By now the strength authorized by the War Department, 1324 officers and enlisted men, is attained. Each of twenty rifle companies has begun its training in accordance with the regulations of the National Guard Bureau, under instructor officers assigned by the Puerto Rican Department of the Army.

It is gratifying to report that in spite of a late start, Puerto Rico is ahead of most States in this work. Only Maine and Delaware have completed their enrollments. I shall ask for the support, during the coming fiscal year, of this work, some $150,000, which will, if all goes well, not need to be used up. We shall, perhaps, not actually call for more than $120,000; but I know that the entire sum will be made available so that any need may be met. You may be sure that under its present leadership the State Guard will always keep in mind the relative poverty of our people as well as the need for home defense.

3. PLANS FOR EMERGENCY

Only in a genuine emergency should I have asked for the use of part of the Emergency Fund. I agree with Governor Leahy([1]) that there has been in the past unjustifiably liberal interpretation of the provisions of law establishing this Fund. It has often been dangerously depleted. Of one thing Puerto Ricans can be certain: destructive hurricanes will return. It required many millions to repair the damage of the last one; and even now, nine years later, less than a million dollars is readily available in the Fund and perhaps half a million of the nominal total of four and one-half million has been put to such uses that it is not recoverable. Whether the people of Puerto Rico have war or peace, the unrelieved threat of hurricane damage need not be allowed to persist. This Fund should be regarded as a kind of insurance, perhaps the only complete kind, for such a disaster. We may work out an orthodox insurance scheme for real properties and even, perhaps, for crops—and we should try to do that—but this will not cover the *jibaro* who is made homeless or the *agregado* who has lost all his possessions. These poorest of Puerto Ricans, until they can reestablish themselves, will need help as they always have. They are not improvident

---

([1]) I refer to his message to the Legislature in February, 1940.

by choice, but because to a family with an income of a few hundreds of dollars a year hurricane insurance is as unattainable as other safeguards against what must seem to them a hostile world. The only chance Puerto Rico has of moving quickly in this matter is to have adequate funds in mobile condition.

There must also be organization. And I digress here, to speak of that. My inaugural day fell in the most critical month of the year in this respect. When I had taken office I began to wonder how Governors could sleep at night during the hurricane season. I not only found the Emergency Fund depleted but no organization (except, of course, the Red Cross) prepared to meet a disaster if one should come. I had fortunately been assigned as Naval Aide, Lieutenant Commander Thomas C. Hennings, Jr., whose wide experience in public life I at once began to use. He was asked to take responsibility for the organization of emergency plans. This he did, and when I was made Director of Civil Defense, he carried on this work as well until Mr. Jaime Annexy was appointed as chairman of a Central Committee for the Island and began intensive organization.

It might have been expected that with all the experience Puerto Rico has had with hurricanes and other disasters, some routines would have been established, some preparations made. There were none. A hurricane occurs about once every ten years on the average. The damage may run as high as a hundred million dollars. Thousands may die or be injured largely from preventable causes—untended wounds, contaminated water, exposure, even starvation. We ought to establish, it seems to me, a permanent emergency organization so that when disaster comes its effects may at least be mitigated.

I propose to protect and augment the Emergency Fund. I asked, at the Special Session of the Legislature in November, that all borrowings should be returned to it. Only part of what I asked was granted. But what has been borrowed for Civil Defense can now be returned, and I ask that that be done. I also ask that there be added to the Governor's staff an officer to be called Director of Emergency Plans, whose duty it will be to have everything in readiness at the time of disaster so that relief may not have to be improvised after the event. That office will not need to be filled for the

124

moment but it should be created against the time when it will be needed. Just now our Civil Defense organization covers the Island and can meet emergencies of peace as well as of war. With the end of war that agency should be kept alive for the purposes of peace. Such an officer on the Governor's staff will serve to do it.

4. We Must Go On With Reform

The problem of civil defense has taken so much of everyone's time and attention during the last months that other problems have been somewhat obscured. It is a mistake to carry this too far. In matters having to do with economic and social betterment, there is no reason for resting. Those who have always opposed progress in these matters would as soon use the excuse of war as any other to take people's minds off injustice and to prevent any change which would threaten their privileges. But those of us who have always worked for changes of this kind would be innocent indeed if we fell into that trap. Protection against the forces of fascism consists not only in fighting it abroad. Its advocates only yesterday were vocal enough at home. And their hearts have not changed. They ought to know that ours have not changed either. And that we are not confused by the new mask of patriotism they wear.

To put it bluntly, we are going to push on—as rapidly as possible—with the social changes which for a generation have been overdue in Puerto Rico. Specifically, we must perfect and enlarge that program of land reform; give workers greater protection; constantly strive to raise the levels of nutrition; make life and living more secure; perfect the devices of government for recruiting and disciplining the public service; plan and execute public work with greater efficiency at the same time that we enlarge it. I shall discuss the specific elements of this program which seem to me feasible at the present time. But at the outset I should like to remind you of the good beginning already made. The Legislature last year set up the Land Authority and Mr. Carlos Chardon, as Director, has begun to assemble his staff and plan his work. It appears that certain changes and amplifications are necessary and these can be made. But the beginning is already substantial.

This can hardly be said of the Department of Labor. Its organization and its operations have in the past been hardly more than a sop to a few troublesome progressives. I am always much more in favor of positive action by government to correct evils than mere regulation. And I would not like to see the Puerto Rico Department of Labor limited to mere regulation. But even on the regulatory side it needs expansion, and certain of its other functions need complete reorganization. For instance, its mediation work. There exists in this field a Commission of which I recommend the abolition, to be followed by the organization, in the Department, of a Mediation Service. This is the method followed in the Federal Department of Labor. There was a time, years back, when inequities in government were thought to be somewhat modified by asking several officials to do what one could do better. That time is past. For such tasks as this, a single headed service is more appropriate.

It may have been some such impulse as this which led the Legislature at the Special Session to set up a Food and Supplies *Commission* rather than the *Administrator* which I recommended in my message on the subject. The experience of several months leads me to recommend even now that this decision be reconsidered. I am sure that a single administrator would be much more effective. The execution of laws is a job for the executive. In this instance it has been impossible for me to move in many ways I should have preferred. A part of the executive was, in other words, handed over to a group outside my control. An administrator who can act quickly and for whose actions I can take the responsibility would be preferable.

In this field, again, of supplies and the control of prices, we cannot at this time be altogether certain of the part which will be played by the Federal Government—probably most of what is necessary, although it did not seem that way last November when the Commission was set up. Bills have now been completed in the Congress which provide, among other things, for the accumulation of stocks of food, for the furnishing of the supplies needed for Civilian Defense, and for the control of prices. The measures taken here can now be regarded as supplementary; and it is a relief to know that the financial burden will in large part be borne by the Federal Government. But here, again, as the Legislature meets, I am unable to speak in quantitative terms. Policies have not yet been made sufficiently precise so that I can advise you how we may accommodate our local organizations to the larger Federal ones. I believe, however, that in setting up an organization for price control and civilian supply and going ahead with certain measures for civil defense, for instance, we have taken steps which will make it unnecessary in these fields to do more than determine what funds will be needed to supplement Federal ones. The basic principles seem to be the same as those which govern the Federal set-up.

The Special Session of the present Legislature last Fall accomplished a great deal, it will be seen, and did it in good time—ahead of corresponding Federal measures. I shall certainly be able to advise you before the end of the session whether changes are necessary. But I think we may take some pride in having been forehanded.

5. The Continuation of the Program

It is impossible, of course, in two years or even four or six to repair the neglect of a generation. It is an especially unhappy circumstance that we must try to do it in the midst of danger which gives a sense of urgency to every task. Certain measures looking toward the improvement of the public service are so basic to any additional expansion in governmental duties that we must pause to work them out even though we wonder why they were not completed years ago and so made available to us now. I refer especially to the setting up of a Planning Board and to the reform of the Civil Service. The one has to do with physical and fiscal accommodation to the means we actually possess; the other to the creation of an efficient service for carrying out whatever policies are determined on. I need not describe the past situation or even that of the present. The Puerto Rican people have aspirations. They know what they want. But everyone knows that the government has no thorough working plans for achieving these aspirations and no way of accommodating our probable income to the tasks we have to do. It was actually necessary last year to pass a so-called anti-nepotism law. This law failed of its effect because it did not cover real nepotism and because it lacked the necessary environment. I propose the substitution for it of a real anti-nepotism act embodied in a reform of the Civil Service to be suggested later.

6. GOOD GOVERNMENT

The truth is that almost all those devices and arrangement which make for good government and have become so familiar in many places, are often lacking, and, when they do exist, are starved for lack of appropriations. That is why, in the midst of emergency and when the machinery of government is especially needed for reform, we have to wait until much of the machinery has been created. We shall never be able to do much with the program of land use or expand our processing industries—at least through governmental assistance—until this work is done. It is for this reason that I propose to you this year the passage of several fundamental measures of this nature: a planning act, which also includes the setting up of an administrative budget; a measure to reform the Civil Service; a bill for the assessment of payments for public improvements; certain bills for the reorganization and modernization of the courts; and measures for the improvement of the police system. There are, of course, other measures which have to do with improvement in the work of the various departments which I shall discuss later. But these are general measures which affect the whole conduct of government. They are basic to its operations everywhere.

Planning is a function which is now seen to be merely the governmental counterpart of that foresight which a business or other organization exercises when it looks ahead to probable resources and desirable functions, except that it has as its ultimate aim the enlarging not of a net profit for the organization but of welfare for the whole people. The desirability of institutionalizing the central controls in any government, of correlating the activities of departments and bringing them into comprehensible relationship not only to each other but to the whole system of government and society, has so commended itself to municipalities that upwards of four hundred effective official bodies of that sort now exist in the United States. They exist also in most states as well as in the Federal Government. The ambition to provide Puerto Rico with a competent planning organization led me last year to consult with a number of Puerto Rican leaders and, with their encouragement, to secure the drafting of a model bill. For this purpose the National Resources Planning Board generously furnished the services of Mr. Alfred Bettman, Chairman for many years of the City Planning Commission of Cincinnati and a distinguished consultant. He has made two extended visits to Puerto Rico and, in consultation with many interested citizens here, has drafted an act which, it is believed, represents the best thought and workmanship which could be brought to bear on our problems. Drafts of this legislation have for some time been circulated among interested citizens as well as among experts wherever they could be found. Many suggestions for change have been made. Some have been embodied in redrafts. The present bill represents that kind of work and thought. It is, in the most genuine sense, non-partizan and non-political and I cannot conceive that any citizen interested in good government can possibly be opposed to its passage.

For some time, as is true in every growing community, the cities of Puerto Rico have had a growing fringe of slums. The positive approach to this problem is, of course, through public housing. And it will be remembered that at the Special Session an appropriation was made for protecting public land from encroachments. But there is more to be done. Not all the slums have grown up on public land. Where they have, measures must be taken to eliminate them; but where private lands are being used in this way, one other method of attack is indicated: assessment for benefit. The worst feature of slums in Puerto Rico is not poor houses, for shelter in itself is not so important as dangerous sanitation; and this is largely a governmental matter. At least it should be. Private owners of land will not and cannot by themselves furnish water, sewer, streets and other necessary facilities. These have to be furnished by government. But the cost must necessarily be assessed largely upon the properties which are served. Lacking a law for this purpose, some owners of property will comply with civilized requirements in these matters and some will not. Some deliberately evade responsibility and allow developments to go on which are a menace to the whole community; but some others are simply unable to meet the requirements. For many decades this problem has been solved in practically all American cities by extending utilities and assessing at least a share of the cost among those served. And indeed there is no other way to prevent the shameful state into which much of San Juan's suburban area has fallen.

As to the use of public land for shack towns, that seems to have been the responsibility of past politicians. As a result much of the surrounding area of the capital city is covered with pitiful and revolting slums. Public housing agencies in Washington have been generous to Puerto Rico. Projects are numerous and well-planned. But the slums have been allowed to grow many times faster than public housing. I have undertaken to prevent, on the one hand, further spread of these abominable areas, and, on the other, to secure even greater aid from Washington. The Legislature made one appropriation for the former purpose at the Special Session —to provide watchmen. Its terms were too restrictive. It should have allowed for fencing and other development. For this I ask amendments now. As to the getting of larger housing appropriations, those were promised, and extensive plans were already drawn, when war began. Since then new policies have been adopted with new terms of which we cannot yet judge the effect. But I have some reason to believe that we can still go forward. It is hoped to do this in such ways as will make the funds go much further—that is to say, make each family unit cost less so that more can be built. If, in just one year we could build more decent houses than were built in the slums, it would be a vast encouragement to everyone and would make our warden service effective. I hope that this next year we may accomplish that. But an essential part of it is the making sure that private properties unserviced by utilities are not used for the erection of shacks. That is the purpose of the proposed law.

The proposed change in the Civil Service is again a matter which is basic to good government. The present system has the appearance of a merit system without accomplishing its more important aims. The best that can be said for it is that it gives some protection to job-holders. This is a virtue, provided the inefficient are not given equal protection with those who are capable and hard-working. But it can scarcely be claimed that the present law makes effectively such discrimination. It was described to me, before I had experience with it, as making it easy to get a job in government and hard to be put out of one. And that is not altogether inaccurate. I propose that instead of the present Commission—which again belongs to a past age in which government was relatively unimportant in the life of a people—there be substituted a Director of Personnel for the government of Puerto Rico together with an appeals board to be substituted for the present Commission. The Director can then be held responsible for selecting, by competitive devices which are by now fairly standardized, and with boards of examiners, new employees of the regular service irrespective of rank. We shall, of course, have to carry out, in connection with this, a complete classification, but this has been long overdue. It has been done recently in the Department of Health by an outside agency, an action which was forced by the requirement of Federal aid; but it is equally badly needed in the other departments. Indeed, it is impossible without it to bring any order or equity into the whole system. But there is no need, if we have an adequately trained and energetic Director of Personnel, of paying an outside agency to carry out such a task. I would urgently ask the Legislature to give this government one able administrator instead of a multiple-headed administrative commission which is sure to waste most of its energy in mutual check-mating. It might be noted that this change could be so managed as to attain the effect sought by the so-called anti-nepotism law which substantially failed to reduce genuine nepotism.

The Attorney General has submitted measures intended to provide a more efficient organization of the Department of Justice and the Judiciary. Of these various measures, I make special mention of the bill authorizing the reorganization of the Municipal Courts, under preparation by a commission created by joint resolution of the Legislature; an amended Juvenile Court Law, having for its aim to provide special agencies to give more attention to youthful delinquents, and a reformation of the Jury Law, which among other changes would grant equal rights to women by including them as jurors.

We should not any longer neglect to improve the condition of the men and women confined in the prison and correctional system. It is well known that women prisoners are housed in a portion of the District Jail of Arecibo; that boys are confined in the District Jails of San Juan and Ponce; that the School for Girls in Ponce operates under the unsuitable name of "Reform School for Delinquent Girls" and has a capacity for only fifty girls; and that the Insular Penitentiary lacks sufficient land for the proper functioning of a dairy farm. Curative measures to meet these situations will be offered for your consideration.

Of interest, not only to the Judiciary, but to other Departments of the Government and the public as well, are matters connected with investigations, traffic cases and the carrying of weapons. It is proposed to provide for a Bureau of Investigation; to organize Traffic Courts to permit of prompt disposition of violations of the traffic laws and ordinances; and to so amend the law as to circumscribe the carrying of weapons. I ask for your favorable consideration of bills embodying these aims.

I mention these matters in this place because of their interest as part of a whole plan to make the government a more effective instrument. In this same connection, I should perhaps call to your attention the lack of cadastral maps and surveys in Puerto Rico, without which it is impossible to carry out accurate and detailed tax work. But these are necessary also for other purposes of government, such as, for instance, planning. And I have hoped that instead of doing this work ourselves at great expense we could devise other ways of accomplishing the same result. That seems to be possible. We are fortunate to have had established here, recently, a regional office of the National Resources Planning Board. Not only for this purpose, but for many others much more important, this contact with Federal planning will have vast results for Puerto Rico. But as to this one necessity, it is probable that a division of this basic work can be made so that the army and navy aerial maps can be used and much of the interpretative work done by the technicians of this Federal office. Our own new Planning Board, if the Legislature accedes to my request and authorizes it, will also share in the work.

Pressure for this fundamental survey work came mostly from the Treasury which could not carry out tax work effectively without it. And a Bill for this purpose, totalling in expense $875,000, was drafted for the Special Session. I took the responsibility then of advising that this expenditure be saved and the result accomplished in other ways. I am willing to continue this responsibility. In the course of a little time I am sure we shall be able to achieve the result. But it may be necessary for you to adopt an enabling act. There are other Treasury projects which are basic. One is the general refunding and reorganization of obligations which I shall discuss more at length, perhaps in a special message or, if we are not ready in time, shall ask you to approve in a later Special Session. Another is a complete recasting of the system of excise taxes. Lack of the one imposes an unnecessary burden of interest; lack of the other raises the cost of living for the poor and fails to achieve the regulating effect which such taxes should have.

7. EDUCATION

I have often spoke of the part which the University ought to play in the life of Puerto Rico. This Island cannot provide for the population to which it is committed unless it undertakes intensive development. And this requires an intellectual center which glows with patriotic flame and renews itself continually with the ardors of its youth. This is not a matter to be desired vaguely; or a value to be attained after all others are achieved. The intelligence directs; it furnishes the means of action. Men without higher nerve centers are beasts. Societies without them are low forms of human association. Not to build up the University, even at the expense sometimes of other activities, is to admit satisfaction with a kind of primitive organization.

The University of Puerto Rico is not sufficiently equipped for the task it has to do. It needs new classrooms, new laboratories, and the like; and I suggest that half a million dollars be allocated for this purpose.(1) It needs new blood in its scientific departments. But even more it needs reorientation. There is too much work of sub-university grade mixed with genuine scholarly effort. And the mixture is good for neither. In the long run we ought to develop several junior colleges elsewhere than on the Río Piedras campus.. And University "reform" which has been so much

(1) I do not here make detailed suggestion for a building program. But so much remains to be done that a beginning can be made almost anywhere. For the present emergency, it would be well to complete the quadrangles at Río Piedras now remaining unfinished, to construct a dormitory for boys and another for girls—these, it must be remembered will pay their own way, or nearly so, from rentals—and at Mayagüez to do certain work, which, if not done at once, will certainly entail much future expense. It might be noted, also, that an appropriation has already been made for an auditorium which lies unused for lack of some necessary addition to it. On the whole west end of the Island there is no meeting place of this sort.

talked about ought not to be longer delayed. The only "reform" worth talking about is what the layman calls "taking the University out of politics", by which he means, of course, exempting it from party change. And the way to do that is the way long ago taken with the judiciary. The governing body now changes with elections. Ex-officio and relatively short-term appointees make it impossible to develop the independence and detachment necessary to a higher nerve center. What is needed above all is a governing body, appointed as is the Supreme Court, by the Executive for an indefinite term. Without this there will be no real "reform". And the University here will never be recognized by its natural supporting agencies—the teachers' and collegiate associations which define standards, the foundations which are so great a help—until this is done. Why put it off?

Perhaps some modification of the customary executive appointment might be devised. The legislature might, for instance, set up a Collegium for supervision of the University, whose membership should change in rotation and whose membership might be large, say fifteen, for instance. The sole duty of such a Board would be to choose three or five trustees for long terms, not all of them changing at once; or it might directly choose the Chancellor. But certain restrictive qualifications might well be established by the Legislature to ensure that trustees were suitable for the great duty of supervising the University; or that the Chancellor was really qualified. The Collegium would meet very infrequently but a seat in it would be a great honor and any citizen would be proud of membership.

The objective of the lower schools is to fit children into a niche in the social and economic scheme. For this reason Puerto Rican education has gone in intensively for vocational education without neglecting to adapt the curriculum to changing needs. Providing adequate facilities for this involves large expenditures. Lacking abundant means, we must adopt such measures as will give us the best possible value from the resources at our command.

We have found centralization of school administration to be desirable, and yet we do not have centralization in a most important branch of that administration—school finances. We still allow certain privileged areas to receive large proportions of municipal monies for school services, while other areas have scarcely any income at all. This situation can only be met by the establishment of an equalization school fund which will give the child in the mountains the same advantages as the child in the rich sugar areas.

There are certain appropriations recommended in the budget bill to extend educational services. These would increase the number of teachers of certain types, particularly of industrial arts, and would provide additional personnel for extending the scope of the work of the Second Unit Schools which have been admired by educators everywhere. They are Puerto Rico's best contribution, so far, to the art of education. They deserve better support.

Throughout the years we have built up a school plant worth some fifteen million dollars. Yet we have done little or nothing to set aside funds to preserve and expand it. I ask that we at long last recognize the need to keep up what we have once created and do it systematically.

There is one problem which always torments educators in Puerto Rico. This is the question of language. It has perhaps been wise to adopt a compromise position. The rich cultural background of the Spanish would be an inestimable loss if the unthinkable attempt were made to substitute another language for it. Yet Puerto Rican youth, especially those who have the talent to enter the managerial class, to become teachers, civil servants—to do all those paper-work tasks which modern society so much depends on—need English too. We are not doing well enough in that, a fault which deliberately shuts off from Puerto Rican youth numerous opportunities to rise in the larger world of which this Island is only a part. It is easy to forget that Puerto Rico seems, in every-day work, like a whole world. But no society of two millions, with such intimate economic exchanges necessary to its life, can afford to act that way.

It was with something like this in mind that I asked the Special Session last Fall to authorize the establishment of a School of Public Affairs in the University, which was done. That will soon be organized and will certainly open new vistas to many young people. What would be said, for instance, if someone should establish an industry in Puerto Rico which would offer more than a thousand jobs at an average of, say, $3,500 a year? He would be regarded as a benefactor in this crowded Island. Yet the Federal government offers exactly

135

such an industry. A Federal official recently showed me a table of those areas which were *in arrears,* in the number of positions occupied in the government. Puerto Rico was first by an immense lead. Preference is given in examinations by geographic areas. Those which do not fill their quotas, however, lose them to others. Puerto Rico, on this list was entitled to 1,148 positions of which only 51 were occupied. There are almost exactly 1,100 positions waiting for young men and women, *with preferential ratings attached.*([1])

Such figures explain the possible usefulness of the new School of Public Affairs which would be, in a sense, a training school for the Civil Service. But, also, they point up our loss from inadequate language teaching. Promising boys and girls are shut out from the largest and most satisfying career open to them if we do not prepare them adequately. And this, of course, neglects entirely the vast field of opportunity to two-language workers in other countries to the South of us. I hope we shall be able to go forward in this field for the sake of a generation which ought not to be confined to the opportunities on this Island any more than this Island should refuse intellectual importations from whatever place they may suitably exist.

8. Police

Unless our Insular police can be put on a different basis, they can never take the place in the community which we all desire. As things are today they are inadequately paid, and they lack security of tenure and certainty of discipline.([2]) Under these circumstances young men of ability will not see in the force a possible permanent career. Moreover, there cannot exist that quick sympathy with the public which is necessary if the police are to be more than mere suppressors of petty crime. In recent difficult situations they have done magnificent work under great difficulties. Everything possible to improve their opportunities ought to be done.

Besides these changes in selection, status and discipline, the Puerto Rican force is far behind in mechanization. It possesses no private communication system such as most other American police now have. And its method of crime detection, for lack of laboratories and trained investigators,

---

([1]) *The Federal Register,* 21 January 1942. P. 440.
([2]) In this connection I recommend the repeal of Act No. 8, approved 5 April 1933, which directs the Governor to proclaim a police-week every year. The police are not appropriately objects of charity.

are almost as much rule of thumb as they were two decades ago. In these matters we shall be able to count on a good deal of Federal aid in one way or another but, of course, we shall have to bear a certain part of the expense. Studies have been made of the cost of setting up a short-wave radio system and it will be included in a budget as soon as that is feasible. It will be necessary, also, to set up a completely new system of districts, based on automotive transportation and radio communication. For this a building program will be needed and should be planned at once. Large amounts are spent every year for the rent of quarters which are almost invariably unsuitable and are often insanitary. New buildings, designed for the purpose and owned by the government will be a long-run economy. It may be that some of them can be so designed as to fit into a fire-district scheme such as is now under study by the Governor's Fire Prevention and Safety Measure Committee. And they ought to make it provide living accommodations for officers on duty there as well as those temporarily assigned. The conditions under which our traveling police now have to find accommodations are a discouragement to that kind of duty.

I am reluctant to suggest any increase in the number of police. I would rather see each policeman fitted out with such equipment and such overhead direction that his efficiency was increased. But examination will show that Puerto Rico will have to make some additions. Nowhere in the United States is there so small a number of police in proportion to the number of inhabitants. Material on this subject will be made available for your study. But I think we dare not wait to make certain increases and certain changes. And I see no reason for waiting longer to establish an academy for the training of recruits.

I recommend, moreover, certain other changes, to remove definite handicaps to discipline and efficiency. The Police Commission ought either to be abolished or to have its duties clearly defined as a Board of Appeals. There have been recently many delays and uncertainties which lead to demoralization. Several changes have been made recently in the force which I think have been received with satisfaction by the public. If together with these changes, a traffic court were set up, as is suggested elsewhere, greatly increased efficiency would result.

137

9. Government in Action

I turn now to measures of a different kind, not to those which improve the whole government service, but to those by which a people achieves its ambitions for progress. In Puerto Rico at this moment these fall easily into two categories: agricultural and industrial (which are mostly processing). There is some possibility of establishing a glass and ceramics industry which, it seems to me, ought to be thoroughly investigated. But primarily the wealth of this Island, which is available in present circumstances and with present knowledge, is agricultural. I would stretch this term to include the catching and processing of fish in the seas around. But how proceed to make the most of these possibilities? It is quite evident that it is not going to be done by private enterprise without more direction or encouragement than in the past. Private enterprise, after many years of complete freedom, has built up a sugar industry about which a damaging admission has to be made: its cost of production is very high and it, therefore, has a competitive power with other areas which is very low. It depends dangerously, therefore, upon a tariff and quota system which might conceivably sometime break down or be disastrously modified. Efficiency in Hawaii and in Florida has increased greatly through the introduction of machinery not used here at all. Puerto Rican efficiency, outside of gains in plant breeding, for which the governmental experiment stations are responsible, has gained very little. Even the production of sugar beets, having gained in efficiency some 25 per cent in the last few years, approaches in cost some of Puerto Rico's cane acreage. Financial institutions and private financiers have had available to them enormous quantities of governmental funds under the peculiar system of financing used by this government in the past. But little has been done with these funds to advance the industrial or agricultural interests of this Island.

These are hard facts to face and I am aware that many Puerto Ricans do not like to be reminded of them. But we shall soon have to see clearly where the real opportunities lie. It should be understood, therefore, that the local financiers of Puerto Rico will not or cannot make those investments and take those risks which are necessary if two millions and more of people are to find the means of making even the barest livings.

138

It is entirely possible, I believe, that the most prosperous year Puerto Rico ever had or will have in the life-times of those now responsible for government, is now behind us. Defense works have, for the past year, been an activity as large as the whole of the sugar industry. In other words, a wholly temporary and factitious element, has, for a year, about doubled Insular income. Suppose that should end— and it soon will—and the activity now being carried on were suddenly reduced by one-half. To put the situation another way: there are now about the same permanent sources of income as existed ten or more years ago; and there are many thousands more people to share them. And there will be more people as time passes. To go on: most of the food for Puerto Rico is still obtained from outside the Island and is paid for by sugar exports. Those exports are almost static in quantity and price. But there are many more people to be fed and the price of food has about doubled. We can improve the distribution of our income but unless its total amount is increased and more opportunities opened, all efforts of this kind will have miniscule results.

No good purpose would be served by pursuing these illustrations. But they are the facts which make outsiders who study our situation impatient and at the same time hopeless. What capital exists is used to no good purpose so far as these problems are concerned. Our growing population seems to economists I have consulted doomed to share a static—or, because of erosion and the depression of tobacco and coffee, a falling—total Insular income. I believe that we can change all this, that we need not submit to the seeming inevitability of economic regression. But it is as clear as crystal that we cannot do it without drastic action, fundamental change. We shall have to direct our energies differently, use our capital for new purposes, reform our habits of consumption. It is a matter really, of taking events in our hands and forcing them to yield better things. Unless we do, many Puerto Ricans must actually starve. I do not exaggerate; and I weigh my words. This is not, however, a time to say anything less than truth.

What is certainly indicated is that government must intervene. It must gather up Puerto Rican capital and help to direct its uses, together with the energy of the people, into channels which will yield livings for all of the two millions on this Island. It is possible that by encouragement and by sharing risks private capital can be induced to undertake projects of this nature. That should be tried. And every effort should be made to do more in the way of pioneering and showing the way. New industries can be brought by government to the pilot-plant stage and the exploitation then shared, sometimes, with private or semi-public capital; or perhaps cooperatives can be encouraged. And there should be an effort to do more in the way of finding basic functional designs for woods, metals, fibres and the like which are native here. The arts of working in these have so degenerated that what little still remains is practically unsalable on outside markets.

Proceeding on this principle of investing government funds and inducing private and semi-public funds to supplement these, in industries which have been explored to the pilot-plant stage and in which design and function have been worked out by the best talent obtainable, Puerto Rico may be made an Island far more independent economically than it is at present. A fisheries industry can be established, a glass, a furniture, a fertilizer, a cotton fabricating, a housing-materials industry, as well as that could be done anywhere. We already have a notable cement plant, which, it will be remembered, was universally condemned by private enterprise and could only be started with government funds. We need more of the same.

Bills will be submitted to you embodying these ideas and possibilities. As I have said before, it is tragic that our government is so ill-prepared to assume these responsibilities and we must proceed with a basically under-trained personnel into a future which has been in no adequate way planned. There are evidently some other things which we must do for ourselves of a service nature. They do not set us forward economically; they are made necessary by the failure of private enterprises to perform functions with which they were entrusted but which are so vital to the community that they cannot be allowed to break down. The time is already overdue when something drastic should have been done to insure better transportation and communication services. But, on the verge of disintegration, it still remains to be done. It must be undertaken, because there is no alternative. We face, especially, in the next few months a crisis in transportation. As everyone knows, automobiles are no longer going to be made and tires will be so few as to be almost non-existent. In San Juan, especially, but also elsewhere, many working people travel back and forth daily, some of them twice daily, from home to work. In the immediate past there has been an unfortunate competition between "públicos" and the bus line which has a supposedly exclusive franchise. This bus line is deep in debt, both to the suppliers of gasoline, tires, etc., and to the Reconstruction Finance Corporation. Its service has worsened month by month. And the "públicos" have illegitimately carried more and more of the passengers. The "público" is not a dependable kind of transport as organized at present. It could hold a legitimate part of the carrying trade if vehicles and tires were available to it and it were organized into cooperatives. But the equipment now in use will wear out quickly and under present conditions is irreplaceable.

The local condition in San Juan is complicated by the existence of an old fashioned trolley line which belongs to the Puerto Rico Railway Light and Power Company. It has been considered something of a nuisance for several years; it will be acquired along with the other properties when the electric services are taken over in the proceedings now going on. All these circumstances taken into account, the best way out seems to me the setting up of a Transportation Authority which will acquire the bus and trolley lines. At the same time, the power to license all other agencies of transportation must be made concurrent. The public could then operate some lines and license others. Under such a system the "públicos", properly organized as cooperatives, could find a legitimate and profitable place in the system without jeopardizing the life of the public bus lines. Unless this is done we shall soon have an inconceivably chaotic situation. Perhaps for this purpose we need to recast and strengthen the Public Service Commission. If so, it should be done at once.

I recommend similar action also in the field of communications. The Insular Government now owns the telegraph and certain telephone lines. By taking over and operating all of them as one integrated system, it could in time provide the kind of service which is expected in these times. In the case

141

of both these recommended Authorities, one consideration is that governmental agencies will certainly be able to command higher priorities for equipment in the months, and perhaps years, of war ahead than could private agencies.

10. Changes in the Water Resources Authority Act

The Puerto Rico Water Resources Authority has now completed its internal organization. The Authority is proceeding as rapidly as possible with the issuance of bonds for development purposes, for purposes of refunding to save interest charges, and for the purchase of properties of the Porto Rico Railway, Light & Power. Co. as directed by the Legislature.

However, a few difficulties have arisen with regard to the interpretation of the Act which have tended to slow down progress in this direction. There are certain defects of expression in the Act, such as appear in almost any law, however expertly drawn. The most important question involved is whether the Authority shall be treated as a bureau of the Insular Government or shall have separate corporate status like the Puerto Rico Cement Corporation, the Tennessee Valley Authority, the New York Port Authority and hundreds of other such corporations set up by governments all over the world. The management of such corporations is put in the hands of their directors without the burdensome managerial restrictions which are usually placed on the management of government bureaus. The Auditor of Puerto Rico holds that under the law, as now worded, practically all the Authority's expenditures are to be made by him, as were the expenditures of the Utilization of the Water Resources... that as far as his intervention is concerned, no change has been made in the status of the system. He is willing to exempt only those expenditures which he exempts for the regular government offices, such as those for wages and for emergency supplies, not exceeding $10 in amount. The Authority has conformed to the ruling of the Auditor, without accepting it.

As to the legal correctness of the Auditor's interpretation of the law I have no opinion. I definitely think that he is doing what he considers to be his duty. He has the support of a preliminary opinion of the Attorney General as to the meaning of the law. But, just as definitely, I believe that any such construction of the Legislature's intent must be based either on an error of interpretation or upon an inaccuracy in the law itself and that the Legislature really intended the Authority to have the same status as other government owned corporations. This status includes power to manage its own affairs and expend its own funds without outside interference by persons not directly responsible for the success of the business. Only thus may it attain the degree of responsibility and efficiency which must characterize the management of successful large scale industrial enterprises. It is mostly to attain this status that the corporate form is used. The presence of the Governor, the Commissioner of the Interior and the Commissioner of Agriculture and Commerce on the Board of the Authority is sufficient to protect the Government's interests.[1]

Under the Water Resources Authority Act, the Insular Government assumes no obligation to pay the bonds of the Authority. The good faith of the People of Puerto Rico is not pledged on the Authority bonds as it was on those issued for the Utilization of the Water Resources. If it is the Authority and its revenues that are to be the primary source of repayment, rather than the Insular Government, then, if only for the protection of the bondholders, the management of those revenues ought to be in the Board of the Authority itself and not in the fiscal officers of the Insular Government. The responsibility to pay debts and the power to manage revenues so that they will be sufficient to pay debts should be vested in the same organization. If the Auditor of Puerto Rico is to control the Authority's funds, then the bonds should be obligations of the Insular Government. If the Authority is to be self-supporting, it must have control over the wherewithal to support itself. In an industrial enterprise, much more than in a government bureau, the power to control expenditures is the power to manage. Intelligent bond buyers know this and will be loath to buy (or will demand higher interest on) the bonds of any corporation that does not control its own money. Therefore, the intention of the Legislature to give the Authority power to manage its own money should be clarified beyond doubt.

[1] In this connection I wish to reiterate an objection I have often made to the membership on the Board of the governor who is far too busy to give the position the attention it needs.

Of course the Authority does not object to a regular commercial type audit, such as those to which all large corporations, governmental or private, are regularly subject. In such an audit a thorough examination of all the accounts, including those of expenditures, is conducted and a critical report is made. It is proposed that such an audit be conducted, and that it be performed by the Auditor of Puerto Rico. It is only to the Auditor's claim of power to decide in advance whether or not particular expenditures are proper that the Authority objects. When the Legislature gave this extreme power to the Auditor, it had in mind no doubt that it should be applied mostly to moneys taken from taxation and not to self-supporting institutions contending with private industry in lively commercial competition.

Doubt has been cast, not only on the Legislature's intention, but also upon its power under the Organic Act to establish a separate government owned corporation. I believe that the Legislature has that power but if, after the Act has been amended to clarify its intention, any doubts as to its power remain, Congress should be asked to remove them by validating the amended bill.

11.   CHANGES IN THE HOUSING LAWS

It is necessary, if we are to proceed expeditiously with a housing program, and to secure approval for projects to be built as part of the defense program, to tighten and simplify the organization. For this purpose I recommend that the various local Authorities, together with the Puerto Rico Housing Authority, be merged in one under the name Puerto Rico Housing Authority and that this organization be given responsibility for planning and managing all Insular housing projects. This change has the approval of those who have the responsibility for housing allocations in Washington and I see no reason for not carrying it out at once.

12.   WELFARE LAWS

I am aware that the prevailing tone of this message is pessimistic. I have to tell you of a vast amount of work to be done. There is no reason why it may not be accomplished. But much of it is extremely technical and complicated. For some tasks of this sort committees have been appointed to study and report. That is true, for instance, of the whole range of legislation in the interest of social welfare, so that, in this whole field we are not yet ready and measures must go over until later. For some others, such as those I have spoken of above, we are perhaps as ready now as we shall be and need not delay. This is especially true of the planning bill which has been prepared with great care. And others are almost equally well studied. There has been some suggestion that in certain fields, such as old age assistance, we may go forward before our commision has reported. I feel that we ought to wait until what is done can be well done.

13. A RECREATION SERVICE

There exists at present a Park Commission in the Department of the Interior whose jurisdiction is quite limited. Its functions have been well performed within its limited scope. But the time seems to me to have come when we should extend to all classes of the people and in many parts of the Island the benefits of professional park and recreational services. Hours of work are being reduced; and even if only in a restricted way, playground and leisure-time facilities suited to our small means ought to be made available. I do not need to enlarge on the benefits which flow from protected play spaces for children of all ages nor the yield of satisfaction from the beauty of ordered park places. These are well enough appreciated by everyone. I have suggested to the proper agencies in Washington that the National Park Service might find in Puerto Rico unique natural phenomena. There is at El Yunque, for instance, the only genuine tropical rain-forest under the flag. It is now under Forest Service jurisdiction, and so reserved without question to the public, but it ought to be managed, in my jugment, by the Park Service. And there are other areas, useful to our teeming population, particularly on the broad beaches, where national parks might well be established. In the meantime, we ought to proceed, with our limited Insular resources, to the acquisition of these areas and their modest adaptation to recreational use.

14. The *Agregado* Program

Title V of the Land Authority Act had to do, it will be recalled, with a program for the betterment of conditions among *agregados* who make up approximately one-half the population of the Island and whose conditions of life are hard. They are mostly farm workers, but few still retain much of the knowledge of agriculture their ancestors had or many of the household arts. For several generations their wages have been so low and their opportunities for work so infrequent that they and their undiminished families —for their fertility seems to have been unimpaired—have been reduced almost to the limits of existence. Most of what is good and beautiful in a material sense has long since disappeared from their households; their state during most of the last generation has been one of bareness, malnourishment and suffering so familiar as to pass for inevitable. It is a high enterprise certainly, perhaps the first duty of each of us, to do what is possible toward breaking the vicious circle here—of disease, hunger and incapacity reflected in a declining ability to make nature yield a living. It was this impulse which actuated the passage of Title V. The Land Authority now proposes a tentative plan for the alleviation of this condition. There is outlined a vast resettlement scheme to be carried out over a period of ten years. I commend this report to the members of the Legislature. I do not agree with its proposals in every detail; I feel, for instance, that many *agregados* ought to be located in cities and towns already organized in which the extension of utilities would be far simpler than in remote areas. But this can still be done and many others will yet remain who work on cash farms who must be provided for. I think, from my experience elsewhere, that costs, even for the simplest facilities, will be far higher than those suggested by the Land Authority, especially when it comes to providing for the utilities. The reason *agregados* can live at all as squatters is that no provision is made for sanitation and that they are parasitic on others for most of their other needs. What they do not get and what their children are deprived of is paid for in the long run by sickness, suffering and early death. But that is hard for a man to understand who has had little education, little even to eat or wear.

This *agregado* program goes to the heart of Puerto Rico. If it cannot, in some degree, succeed, all our work is wasted. To try to establish a middle class upon a foundation of abject poverty is to build on betraying sand which will some day overwhelm all society. We must clear the slums out of the country-side just as we must clear them out of El Fanguito and La Perla. Whether the resources for this vast task exist is less a matter of something fixed and natural than of human managerial ability. Foods, fibres, woods—all that comes out of the ground—grow here all year round. Our resources per acre are perhaps four times those of the temperate zones. We are rapidly learning to use our water power for the public benefit; and wind power will be next. The limitations of Puerto Rico exist far more in men's minds and in their organization than in any rule imposed by nature. These we can improve. And I propose that we do not begin our reconstruction with lamentation but rather with courage. We shall have to change much and disturb ourselves greatly. The results will be richly worth the cost.

15. AMENDMENTS TO THE LAND AUTHORITY ACT

Certain amendments to the Act passed last year are now suggested by the Land Authority. Since the primary responsibility for the program is theirs, these suggestions should be received in good spirit and carefully considered. One of the important ones (Section 24) has to do with changes necessary to secure the advantage of funds possessed by the Farm Security Administration and available for use in our program but not precisely in the ways laid down in the original Act. There is involved no significant change of policy which should prevent adoption of this amendment and I recommend that it be accepted. I also recommend that provision be made for the establishment of demonstration farms, managed by the Authority itself. This will incidentally enable us to proceed with the further liquidation of the P.R.R.A. agricultural program without giving up any of its really essential services. But more importantly it will, if well managed, set up centers from which better strains of livestock and approved seed stocks can be disseminated by exchange or by sale.

Certain other amendments are suggested which have the effect of clarifying its meaning and making its terms more precise. The Authority should have the power to fix salaries —that is part of the nature of an Authority. The amendment which removes the possibility of sale to the managers of proportional benefit farms is one which ought to be approved without question. If such disposal were to be made of these properties a situation would be created similar to that at Lafayette where a few colonos were set up in very profitable businesses and little consideration was given to the other parties at interest. This would be the most inexcusable turn our land reforms could take since it would inevitably shut out from benefits about 95 per cent of the people. It is not for five per cent of the more well-to-do farmers that all these years of effort to change Puerto Rico's land system have been undergone. And this ought never to be lost sight of in the confusions of the moment. We have set out to better, even if only a little, the conditions of those who have suffered the bitterest of fates and to open new opportunities for their children. Nothing should divert us from this purpose. We may lack a good deal, as we progress into the program, of equipment and efficiency; we shall have to learn by doing. But that is inevitable. There is such a thing as keeping hold on permanent values and reducing temporary inefficiencies and oppositions to their proper place. We shall have to cultivate it.

16. HEALTH ACTIVITIES

In spite of recent temporary amelioration in some sections of the Island, the prevailing unemployment and low incomes result in economic distress among large masses of our population, which is conducive to poor health and deplorable conditions. If we consider also the widespread prevalence of certain tropical diseases, notably malaria, hookworm and dysentery, in addition to tuberculosis, the seriousness of social and health problems on the Island is evident.

Malaria control work is being carried out intensively in the neighborhood of several army camps in order to protect the health of the armed forces. To meet the anticipated need of an expansion of hospital facilities during a period of emergency, the Insular Health Department, in cooperation with the W.P.A., is training nursing auxiliares and other emergency hospital personnel. By an act of the Legislature the land and buildings of the old Quarantine Hospital were transferred to the Federal Government for national defense purposes. A modern institution for the isolation of contagious patients is being constructed by the W.P.A. in the neighborhood of the Bayamón District Hospital. Funds required for the equipment and maintenance of this hospital have been included in the proposed budget for the next fiscal year.

Act No. 29, approved on July 20, 1935, provides for the construction and maintenance of four district hospitals to be operated by the Insular Department of Health with the advice of a Territorial Charities Board, for the care of the underprivileged population. Three of these hospitals have been adequately equipped and are in full operation. Two of these have been already included in the approved list of the American Medical Association and the American College of Surgeons. The equipment for the fourth hospital located in the Aguadilla district has been purchased and is being delivered. Although on July 1st, 1943 there will be sufficient revenues from legislation already approved for the maintenance of these four district hospitals, it is necessary that the amount of $300,000 be appropriated for the maintenance of the Aguadilla District Hospital during the fiscal year 1942–43.

Since the present plan contemplates the construction and operation of seven district hospitals to cover the Island's needs, I am taking the necessary steps to secure Federal assistance in the construction and equipment of at least three additional hospitals to be located in the Mayagüez, Ponce and Guayama districts.

The recommendations for appropriations for salaries in the Department of Health are presented in lump sums for the several bureaus and institutions instead of being itemized by positions, as heretofore. This is because a classification of the positions in that Department is in process and the details are not yet known. The classification work will be finished shortly and lists of the positions and their proposed salary rates, in accordance with this classifications will be presented for your information.

This classification and compensation plan which is one of the requirements of the Social Security Law, was undertaken upon request of the Federal agencies controlling social

149

security funds, which last year contributed in the amount of $793,300 to the program of the Insular Health Department.

It is, thus, highly important that the Legislature make its appropriations for salaries for the Department of Health in such a way as not to retrict the application of the classification plan. Rigid "line item" appropriations by individual positions would be incompatible with the application of the compensation plan and would jeopardize the Island's further participation in the social security funds.

17. AGRICULTURE

Puerto Rico lives from the soil. Nothing much in the way of other industry has yet—though much better efforts must be made—been established. But for hundreds of years the soil has yielded first one, then another, crop which has absorbed the work of the people and given them back a living. It has not always—not even often—been a good living for the workers. And, strangely enough, in such a generous all-year environment, most of the food came from outside. Rice, beans, codfish—this is even now, as it was a hundred years ago, the standard diet. It was made standard by hard masters of the land because it was cheap. It would keep, and it came as return cargo from the ports to which the ships carrying Puerto Rican products went. It was not a good diet. But a tropic sun, mangoes in season, a tiny seed which flavors the potful of rice—the achiote—and other fruits and vegetables, used sparely, supplied a tolerable nutritive balance.

So people lived and multiplied. There are those still living who can recall the great days—as they seem now—of the sugar, coffee, tobacco era. Each of these was a famous crop: sugar for the flat lowlands, tobacco for the elevated interior valleys, coffee for the hills. The story of decline for coffee and tobacco is a tragic one. Many Puerto Ricans have always felt that the best of their people, the genuine old culture, lay in the hills. A special sentiment surrounded coffee growing, and, to a less degree, the cultivation of tobacco. There is still coffee in Puerto Rico and still tobacco. But a combination of circumstances has surrounded their cultivation with greater and greater difficulties. Coffee suffered from cheaper, more prolific varieties, growing in competing

150

countries. It suffered, too, from being inside rather than outside the high-wage economy of the United States—so long as coffee was unprotected by any tariff. And even now with quotas and subsidies, the handicaps are scarcely equalized. It was a traditional industry and took reluctantly to changed methods and new varieties. And so there is trouble through all the coffee country.

With tobacco it was worse. The best areas have been exhausted and cultivation has been pushed back onto steeper and steeper slopes, with almost no attention, until just recently, to the ravages of erosion. So that thousands of once fertile acres are now ruined. But Puerto Rican tobacco was cigar tobacco anyway, and the world took to smoking cigarettes. What with losses of markets and losses of soil, there is trouble all through the tobacco country, too.

When disasters like this happen, those who suffer from them always feel a sense of grievance. And indeed nothing that has gone on has been more than partly the fault of those in the industry. But public policy has to be shaped in view of inevitables. What is dying cannot forever be kept alive. The human results of change can be mitigated, but such vast movements as are affecting coffee and tobacco are outside the power of Insular legislators. A certain part of the coffee and tobacco industries can, by wise planning, be kept alive. Farmers who let their soil run away on tobacco-planted hills, or who will not adopt new coffee varieties hurt themselves more than any public help can ever repair. And public sympathy and assistance ought to be reserved for those who have a chance of pulling through because they are honestly trying their best.

The Federal government and the Insular government, working together, have done nobly, it seems to me, in their attempts to check the decline of coffee and tobacco. I will not recall here the various measures taken, the funds devoted to this purpose. I will simply remind you that there are reasons why we should go on trying. To equalize such costs of production as are traceable to higher wages here, is merely to relieve our workers from a competition in low standards which we could not afford in the long-run anyway. We ought to try to get standards raised in other places rather than lowered here. But the mere payment of subsidies is, of course, not enough. There is no concealing the fact that deficits in one place have to be made up in another. If one industry receives a subsidy another has to pay it. To deny endlessly the forces working against an industry and to refuse trial of all other alternatives is likely to end in disaster. For, as I have so often pointed out, our present great crop, sugar, is "political". It, too, is subsidized. And to ask it to bear in turn a subsidy for the Island's two other main crops is to base our economy on uncertainty.

Nor is such a situation necessary and inevitable. It is a fact that some coffee, some tobacco, and a good deal of sugar is grown under conditions which would allow them to compete with any regions in the world. This is sometimes because of superior management, sometimes because of highly productive soil and other growing facilities. For whatever reason, we can grow some coffee, some tobacco and a good deal of sugar with complete assurance that no one can beat us at it. That infers a certain amount of unprofitable effort (in the economic sense) which might possibly be better directed. I do not believe the Puerto Rican government nor even the Federal government can—or should—keep everyone in coffee or tobacco who happens to make that choice, regardless of his managerial ability or the productivity of his soil. And then, of course, these factors change. Soils which once were profitable may erode, farms may fall into careless hands. There was once a ruthless way of eliminating these farms and these men. When they could no longer pay their debts, the men were eliminated and the farms were put to other uses. This seemed harsh and it was. And the matter of foreign competition was traded on. So government intervention began, first as tariff, later as outright subsidies.

We have, however, to keep our minds on what it is we are trying to do. We are not (or ought not to be) trying to protect carelessness and inefficiency. We are trying to protect our workers against competition with ruinous wages elsewhere and our farmers against fortuitous circumstances which are legitimately temporary. There cannot be objection either to the use of government as an instrument for achieving what has come to be called "parity"—that is a general market disadvantage among agricultural products as compared with others. But these legitimate interferences we have to separate out from the others—the protections to

152

inefficiency and carelessness. An Island like Puerto Rico can afford these last far less than a richly rounded economy which is half industrial.

I call attention to these facts in order to define policy. I was asked recently to approve a bill which would have given a blanket subsidy to coffee *exporters*. It seemed to me necessary to disapprove, since this was an example of that kind of law which, without discrimination, hands over sums from the public treasury without requirements for compliance. It had the added repugnant feature of not even mentioning workers or farmers. But it was in any case illustrative of the kind of thing we should not do.

The coffee plan now in effect is not wholly satisfactory. But it is far better than the one suggested. My own preference, following the reasoning I have outlined, is for a different long-run attack, meanwhile keeping the present legislation in force. If we are going to subsidize further, let us subsidize new crops which may succeed, not old ones which in so many places cannot again be profitable. I do not suggest that we neglect the needs of coffee and tobacco farmers and workers. But I suggest that while we give this kind of relief, we begin another kind of regenerative action. I shall send you separate communications concerning each of these industries before the session is over. The legislative commission on coffee has been at work and you will have the benefit of its advice. I hope we may find really wise measures in both these instances for very hard problems.

There are thousands of acres of upland in Puerto Rico which were once valuable for high-producing crops and are now almost abandoned. The top soil is mostly gone. But trees of many very useful kinds, and perhaps vines, will grow there. What I propose is the development of these lands not in old ways but in new ones. Something like this is being done now in Haiti with notable success and with capital from the American Export-Import Bank. A similar scheme for Santo Domingo and for other countries is in the making. Why not Puerto Rico? There are many crops available to us, if we take a realistic view of present values, which we have always said we could not grow. Tobacco or coffee land once worth a good deal may now be devoted to teak, quinine, mahogany or similar forest woods. It will

153

require great changes. A crop can be had only once or twice in a generation and meanwhile workers will have to be supported. That is one reason why it is appropriately a government risk.

Then there are the new termite-proof bamboos which are shorter crops but which need to be made available, by new designing, for furniture and other building uses. There are essential oils, spices, probably grapes, and sea-island cotton. There is rubber . And there are oil-bearing trees of many kinds. I might mention many more, known to be possible on land not too valuable, and risky, perhaps, as dependable crops. But funds sunk in unprofitable subsidy—always keeping in mind that I refer to the unprofitable parts of the production—might far better be used to develop possible new additions to our economy.

I believe, however, that we may find funds for some sizeable demonstrations. If a development corporation can be set up in Haiti outside the United States, there ought to be good argument for setting one up in a territory of the United States. At any rate I intend to ask that it be done. And I shall perhaps request a little later that it be authorized by law.

I turn now to certain other matters which have to do with the continuing of profitable activities now being carried on by the Department of Agriculture and Commerce. The tick eradication campaign, which is so important, will not be completed this year. It is necessary to eradicate every last tick if we are to be free of Texas fever which more than anything else prevents the successful raising of animals. And, once free, we shall not have to do more than maintain a quarantine. We also have the possibility of eliminating contagious abortion. I am sure you will see the necessity of supporting this work. As for soil conservation, it is perhaps hardly necessary to argue that in order to get ahead we should supplement the work of the Federal Soil Conservation Service. There is general awareness now that Puerto Rico's soil, her richest resource and main reliance, is wasting away at a frightening rate. As the soil is lost on the slopes, the people too, are washed down into city slums, there to be a growing problem to be met with diminishing resources.

It is perhaps appropriate to close this message to a wartime Legislature on this note. As we fight for democracy we fight also for human improvement. I am confident that you as legislators will do your part in both the ongoing struggles of mankind.

R. G. TUGWELL,
Governor.

LA FORTALEZA, *February 10, 1942.*

The war was foremost in the legislator's minds. They acted accordingly. They smoothed out Civilian Defense, making it more efficient. They created a State Guard to replace National Guard units absorbed into the army. They established an Insular Fire Service to protect property against air raids. They appropriated money for control of malaria around military camps. They declared a war emergency and established a Development Company with authorization to take over and operate any industry forced to suspend because of war conditions. They recognized the mistake they had made in the Food and Supplies Commission and gave the Governor the Administrator he had originally asked.

The legislative action was not confined to the war. Preparations also were made for the peace which was to follow. The Development Company was directed to encourage new industries, and a Development Bank was established to finance it if the Legislature should later decide that would be desirable or necessary. A Planning Commission was created to assess Puerto Rican possibilities and to guide economic change. The University was reorganized to take it out of partisan politics. A Transportation Authority was set up to take over the San Juan bus line, in which the Reconstruction Finance Corporation had already invested heavily. A Communications Authority was established to take over the Government-owned telegraph system, which for years had operated at a deficit, and the Puerto Rico Telephone Company whose charter provided for its eventual return to the Government. The sugar industry was declared a public utility, open to regulation by the Public Service Commission. Enabling legislation was passed to permit the Farm Security Administration to cooperate in a greater distribution of land under the insular Land Law. The law governing the Minimum Wage Board was amended to require the board to make wage studies in specific industries upon the Governor's recommendation. A Parks Service was created as a nucleus for future recreation. New restrictions were placed on child labor.

Not all that the Governor proposed was approved. The Personnel Director and Appeals Board he urged as a substitute for the antiquated Civil Service Commission was denied him. Governmental machinery for the improvement of housing, essential to elimination of Puerto Rico's slums, was improved, but the Governor's recommendation for merging

157

insular and local housing authorities was not accepted. Funds were provided for food planting, and for control of the cattle tick. But the Governor's recommendation for a study of non-productive coffee land as a prelude to turning it to other uses was lost. The Water Resources Authority law was amended to remove the Authority from the restrictions of governmental pre-audit, but the Legislature did not accept the Governor's proposal that he be removed from the Authority board.

Also neglected were a whole series of governmental reorganizations which the Governor wished to modernize the municipal courts, make women eligible for jury duty, open special courts for traffic cases, level inequalities in the distribution of monies to public schools, reform the Police Commission and enable the Insular Treasurer to carry on refunding operations administratively.

As the war advanced, it tightened its grip on the island. Enemy submarines menaced ships bound for Puerto Rico with food. The Governor, from his improvised bedroom on the roof of old Fortaleza, anxiously watched supply boats enter and leave San Juan harbor. For months he had tried to persuade the island to plant its own food; for months sugar planters opposed him, saying they always could get enough ships. Business men, still secure in the notion that they could do business as usual, were bringing in luxuries in space which could have brought food. In May, there was a conference in Jamaica of Supply Officers from the British and American islands of the Caribbean. To it came a warning message from the State Department, concurred in by Army, Navy, Interior and Agriculture. The Governor went at once to Washington to see whether help could be had from the Federal government to ease transition to the war economy which sugar planters and merchants were resisting. When he came back, he explained over the radio what must be done.

RADIO MESSAGE
LA FORTALEZA,

I do not think that anyone who has not for a time shared the responsibility of being Governor of Puerto Rico can know the lift in a Governor's heart as he sees from the wall of La Fortaleza ships coming and going through the passage at the entrance to the harbor of San Juan. This free going of ships furnishes the means; and the coming of ships brings the materials of life, to Puerto Rico. And a Governor lives by the life of the people. For most of our food, for most of our building materials, and for our other necessary supplies we are dependent upon the outside world. Never in the history of Puerto Rico has this safe coming and going of ships been threatened as it is threatened now. Never has there been such danger of the economic strangulation which would follow upon the closing of our ports.

Puerto Rico is not suffering, at least as yet, the kind of disaster which came on December 7th to Hawaii. Thanks to the vigilance of the Island's defenders such a disaster has become less and less likely as the months of war have passed. Puerto Ricans have seen the transformation of their Island from a defenseless outpost to a strong fortress within an incredibly short time. We do not need to be unreasonably afraid that any enemy is likely to overpower us. No one can make any certain predictions in a matter of this kind. The war has touched the most unlikely regions of the world before now and it must always be remembered that we are one of the main guardian bastions for the Canal which crosses the Isthmus of Panama. But just now, at least, and for the immediate future, that is not the greatest concern of those who are entrusted with the defense and the welfare of Puerto Rico.

There is another menace and one which in a way is just as serious. I mean, of course, the submarines of the enemy which in the last few months have infested the waters of the Caribbean, the South Atlantic and the Gulf of Mexico, doing great damage to our commerce and stopping the free passage of ships upon their regular routes of commerce. The Governor can stand now upon the parapet of La Fortaleza and see more war ships and troop ships coming and going than merchant ships bringing food and materials needed for con-

161

struction and taking away the sugar, the molasses, the coffee, and the tobacco with which we pay for the things we buy.

This is not a problem for Puerto Rico alone but is a problem which affects other Islands in the Caribbean and even those nations which surround it. Those who are most self-sufficient, not those who have the greatest export crops, are, for the moment, the most fortunate, since they can at least live cut off from the rest of the world.

These dangers and tensions have been growing in recent months and I, as Governor, have, of course, been aware of them and working for their solution. A few weeks ago it was determined by officials in Washington and in London to call at Jamaica a meeting of the supply officers of all the British and American Caribbean islands to assess the situation and to find out what could be done. There was transmitted to this meeting as a part of its instructions a directive which was joined in by the responsible departments in Washington which indicated that for the immediate future Puerto Rico would have even fewer ships than in the past and that measures must be suggested to Washington which would increase local food supplies and to insure against such losses in the American areas as were preventable.

After this meeting, at which the irreducible quantities of supplies for the various areas were surveyed, I thought it my duty to go to Washington and confer with various officials to see whether the recommendations I had made could be carried out at once. These recommendations were calculated on my part to insure that no one should go hungry and, as far as possible, that no one of our farmers or our merchants should suffer economic losses either now or in the future.

The most fundamentally important of them, of course, had to do with the insuring of such a supply of foods and medicines and then, if possible, a supply, even if a reduced one, of such building and other materials as are necessary to prevent unemployment from coming upon us all at once. In order to do this it was necessary to have the generous and loyal cooperation of many officials in Washington in the War and Navy Departments, the Departments of Interior and Agriculture, in the War Shipping Board, and the War Production Board, and this cooperation was given, actually, in a measure which in all my years of experience as a public official I have never before seen. Everyone was sympathetic to the position of Puerto Rico and everyone wanted to do everything possible to help.

First let me describe to you, in a few words, what is being done to insure the steady flow of necessities for the people of Puerto Rico regardless of the intensification of submarine activity and regardless of the increasing necessity for the use of all the ships that can be got together for supplying the fighting fronts. The Agricultural Marketing Administration for the Department of Agriculture has allotted generous funds with which to purchase large stocks of food and another fund is in the possession of the officials of the Department of the Interior which can be used for the purchase of other necessities. Up until now it has not seemed necessary to concentrate the buying of supplies in a single agency which would act for all Puerto Rican merchants. That is apparently going to be necessary in the immediate future. I was told that it will not be possible to go on in the old way, which resulted in such ships as were available coming to us with supplies not urgently needed at the moment, or goods which could be said to have the character of luxuries in times like these. The War Shipping Board has told us that the wastes and inefficiencies of the past must be corrected; that we will be allotted only the ships necessary to carry essential materials here; and that we must accommodate ourselves to this situation. They are not doing this in any other than a spirit of patriotism and generosity. They say that they can give us shipping enough so that all our essential needs can be supplied if we will use those ships to the greatest advantage and if we will adopt trade routes safer than those now in use. For this purpose the Agricultural Marketing Administration has already stationed agents in new parts of the world from which we have never before had materials. They will buy for Puerto Rico and other Caribbean islands. They are already purchasing food and ships are already being loaded. Besides this trains are rolling southward in the United States toward ports of embarcation. These food supplies will come to Puerto Rico by a safe route, partly over-land, under the protection of the Army and the Navy and they will insure us against the worst hazards of the present submarine menace. You will understand why I cannot describe it to you in detail. But you may take my word for it that this ensures

163

Puerto Rico against the worst consequences of the submarine blockade. This is what I felt must be done first and most certainly because it affects working people, the *jíbaros* and *agregados* who, because their wages are low and their houses small, have laid by no stores of food. For their sake the merchants' shelves must not be allowed to be empty.

To the people of Puerto Rico we say that their Government stands by them in these trying times. War has reached our shores and the enemy lurks in the Caribbean. Let us all face the hard facts with the patriotism and loyalty characteristic of our Island.

The people understood the message for what it was, a protest against selfishness. The Governor's desk was heaped high with telegrams of public confidence. Next night he was on the air again, explaining what he was working for in Washington. It was fortunate that he did this, for months later he was to be accused of failing to do it—accused for political reasons by the very people who were obstructing his efforts.

I have told you what is being done to insure the food supply even with the submarine blockade shutting us off from the world; of the plan for buying foodstuffs especially in single great orders and distributing them to merchants as they arrive.

I want, now, to go on to tell you of two other measures. These are being undertaken for the sake of those same small people I spoke of before: the workers and the farmers. These are most vulnerable to the cruel forces at large in a warring world. One of these measures has to do with the W.P.A. It was peculiarly unfortunate for us that war plans called for cutting down the enrollment just now. And I have undertaken to explain to officials of the W.P.A. in Washington that our situation is the reverse of that which prevails in the States. Up there, some unemployment exists because certain kinds of industry are shutting down. But so many war industries are enlarging that employment is available somewhere within reach of almost everyone. Indeed the need is so great that many women are taking jobs formerly held by men. Here, the submarine blockade is making materials for construction hard to get; we cannot get many new machines or much motor transport; and gasoline and fuel oil are as scarce as food. This means that the Army and the Navy, especially, are going to have to cut down their projects and that private and public building cannot go on. We are going to have unemployment. But we must control it as far as we can.

What will be the use of the stocks of food we are working so hard to get if men are out of work and cannot buy them? They will be of no use, of course. And we must not let such a thing happen if we can prevent it. Two obstacles stand in our way. First, there is the danger that W.P.A. will actually be eliminated or severely reduced. I have argued that it ought to be enlarged in Puerto Rico and I believe that actually it will be. I have also undertaken to have modified an order of the War Production Board which prevents the construction of projects of more than $500 value. This order is in effect all over the nation. I have argued that, in our special case, any construction work should be allowed which does not require priorities—which does not use material needed for war purposes. This is what the order was for: to save precious materials needed for planes, ships, tanks, and guns. I would not ask for any favor at the expense of helping in this. But where no such result is involved we might well be allowed to build.

If we can have these two modifications—enlargement of W.P.A. and relief from the order which prohibits construction with local materials, the employment crisis can be met with more confidence. It is my hope that these changes will be made by the time our stringency actually arrives.

Aside from that, as you already know, the Federal Government has already undertaken to keep prices at a stable level—not at one which will be ruinous to merchants, but one, nevertheless, which will protect those who must buy goods moving to us through seas afflicted with enemy submarines.

I turn now to the situation of farmers and estate owners especially those who have the larger operations. When I was told that we should not have enough ships to move the current crop or the crop planned for next year, I for one took means to find out if this was substantially a military order. I was told that it was a military matter and one of extreme urgency. It must be realized that the United States is building bases all the way from Jamaica and Bermuda to the Guianas on the coast of South America, and that with the responsibility for these bases, there goes a certain responsibility for people. On most of the islands—as in Puerto Rico—export crops are grown extensively; and none of them grows enough food for nearly all the needs of its people.

To military men who must take care of the bases and who feel responsible for the civilians, too, it has seemed a simple proposal that sugar lands be converted to growing food. Actually it is not so simple; and the objections to it as a policy are numerous and well-founded. But, in this emergency, the demand must be met. There is no alternative. It was at first argued that most of the sugar land in Puerto Rico could be devoted to the growing of food crops. That, of course, was out of the question and was not seriously insisted on for long. There is, however, an insistence on the use of some of the best lands for growing food. And this demand cannot reasonably be opposed because it is perfectly feasible. It will take considerable quantities of seed and fertilizer and some machinery; but it is quite possible to do; and indeed it is the other side of the total program which we must adopt if we are to defeat the purpose of submarine warfare. On the one hand we shall bring in necessary food; on the other we shall grow our own—or as much as we reasonably can.

It was against considerable opposition that I urged the point of view that such a program ought to be undertaken only after adequate compensation was given. It was said that there was sufficient compensation in two very compelling motives; first, that the produce would be bought by a government agency at a guaranteed price and, second, that it was a patriotic matter to do it anyway. Our farmers would be growing food for Puerto Ricans who otherwise might not have it. That these were compelling motives I did not deny. Nevertheless I felt that if the sacrifice were made and sugar lands or potential sugar lands were turned to food crop growing, compensation might well be given. And I believe that this view will prevail. In your newspapers you have already seen evidence of progress in this matter. The President has taken the first step in providing the necessary funds.

I think it will be found that the Washington officials who will be in charge of this program will approve substantially the same compensation for the growing of food as was formerly given for the growing of sugar. I believe that if necessary it will be given as a subsidy. The plan is being worked on now in the Department of Agriculture in Washington and farmers will soon be called into consultation to work out its further details. I have already conveyed to Mr. Dickey, of the Sugar Producers' Association, its broad outlines and have asked for assistance in perfecting its operations. I believe that they will cooperate generously and patriotically.

The present plan for subsistence crops will go ahead as planned. And small farmers as well as large will share in the benefits of the new scheme.

I have often discussed with friends in Puerto Rico and elsewhere the difficulties and dangers of the one-crop agriculture to which Puerto Rico is committed. I do not know the way out of all those difficulties and dangers. I have, in this instance, taken every precaution available to me to make certain that the present emergency should not be used to Puerto Rico's disadvantage in the later settlement of a permanent policy. I do not believe that if we turn a certain proportion of our potential sugar land to the growing of food it will be counted against us in future days of peace. The question of quotas will some day have to be discussed again and we shall be in competition for their enlargement with other areas. There is no disposition on the part of anyone to whom I have talked to use the present situation for gaining an advantage. I only speak of it because I have heard it used as an argument. If we set against this contention the fact that, unless we do intensify our food growing, we shall be endangering the food supply as well as failing to do our part in the war effort, I cannot believe that anyone will find it in his heart to refuse cooperation.

The program I have outlined to you is one which requires changes. Merchants must, to a certain extent (though I believe not harmfully) modify their habitual ways of carrying on their trade. The sugar growers who have a prejudice against any other kind of cultivation must sacrifice their prejudices in the emergency. Those who work must trust me and the other officials of their government as we endeavor to prevent unemployment and secure their food supply. I hope that these may be all the sacrifices Puerto Ricans will be called upon to make. For the merchant there is the fact that he can still carry on his customary work. For the farmer and the estate owners there is the possibility of generous payment for the growing of food. For the worker there is the assurance that the crisis which we had hoped to avert until after the war, and which is now likely to come upon us at once, may be substantially lessened by public work and, if necessary, relief.

There are other aspects of the whole plan to meet the crisis of war. We shall use alcohol made from molasses to replace partly the gasoline which is so scarce; we shall turn the rest of our molasses into the rum which yields so great a revenue. These will help. And there are numerous other arrangements in the making. All of them require of you as well as of me, some work, some sacrifice, some restraint under provocation.

Of these matters I shall speak to you further tomorrow evening. Hasta mañana!

170

For a second successive day telegrams heaped the Governor's desk. The people were glad to know what he had told them. He went back to the radio on the third night to name those responsible for delaying the Governor's program and to say why they were doing it.

RADIO MESSAGE
LA FORTALEZA,

The People of Puerto Rico know well enough that I am not new to public life. They know that I served through the early years of the New Deal in Washington and they know that I served after that with a progressive administration in the City of New York. I have always felt that they know, also, what that means, and that I had no need to make further explanation of my attitudes.

It is by now a fairly long service. During it I have learned that he who works for progressive causes is never left to carry out his service in peace. Those who fear that they may lose money or power never contemplate giving them up without a struggle. They almost invariably attempt to destroy those who are thought to cause their troubles. But the people of Puerto Rico know this well enough too. I do not need to explain. It may be useful, however, if I say, what they may not know, that I shall never be confused, any more than they, by attempts to create confusion. I can assure them too that I shall never be the kind of person who thinks of himself as the *cause* of change. I am only one of its *agents*. And there are many Puerto Rican leaders just as useful—far more useful—in carrying out indispensable reform. And they have been working for you far longer than I.

No one man, not even the President himself, *caused* the New Deal in Washington. Forces larger than any of us, larger than all of us, were destroying the old order and creat·ing the new. That process might alternatively have been orderly and decent or revolutionary and bloody. It turned out to be orderly and decent because opposition ceased at the danger point. And I am sure that will be true also in Puerto Rico. There is no need for fear.

It was the genius of President Roosevelt to accept conditions as he found them and to recognize that America's chance of survival, of growth and prosperity, lay in making, boldly, deep and broad changes throughout the whole social structure. He did not hesitate, when it was necessary, to carry through these orderly changes vigorously. He fought when fighting was the only way. He was always opposed to any kind of violence and any unnecessary departure from customary ways. But he meant to secure the American future, and he did. The New Deal has gone on now in the Federal sphere for some nine years. It has become embeded in our customs. Only the most ultra reactionary any longer questions the justice and the rightness of those laws for which the President was called such abominable names throughout the early stages of reform.

The New Deal never properly came to Puerto Rico in those years. Puerto Rico was always somewhat detached, isolated from the currents of change. Most of the Island's people remained sunk in helpless poverty. The efforts which were made to lift her out of this morass through the Puerto Rico Reconstruction Administration and other New Deal agencies were more or less successfully defeated, one after another, by the small group of reactionaries who dominated the economic and political life on this Island. They were able to keep their little kingdom pretty much intact from the forces which were at work elsewhere. To this effort they devoted great cleverness, large sums of money, and a vicious willingness to destroy any individual who seemed to threaten their power. Most of them made the mistake, however, that reactionaries have made throughout history: they refused to give away a little that they might retain much. Most of them refused to become, as they might have done, leaders of a new order in Puerto Rico, a regime devoted to the welfare of the people, to economic betterment, to social justice, and insisted with every means at their disposal on fighting bitterly against even the suggestion of change.

Fortunately there were exceptions. The leaders who stand out today as people's champions have been tried in hard battle, and they are true. I suggest that there is nothing unusual about this, nothing new, and nothing strange except perhaps that so many intelligent people should so long and persistently have resisted the lessons being forced upon them. And not only were the lessons forcibly taught; they were pointed up by Puerto Rican progressives over and over again. But the trend was inevitable. History had her way with Puerto Rico as she has had her way with one after another of the reluctant areas of the world.

I say these things to you so that you may understand that I, no more than you, am likely to be confused by fictions and artificial turmoil. I know as well as you do that such agitation do not go below the surface and have no support among the people. That you will not be confused has been amply demonstrated by the support in your Legislature for measures similar to those which have been found necessary elsewhere in a period like this. I speak to you as I do not at all because I think your minds need to be cleared; and not even very much because I am afraid that you may think mine needs to be cleared; but because, added to the passions which are associated with economic change, we now have an entirely new reason for division: the war.

War has sometimes seemed, to those who oppose progress, a very fortunate thing, since they have felt that if, under its special circumstances, they could create sufficient disturbance, set group against group, they might frighten lovers of order and find a refuge for themselves in martial law. They have thought, in fact, to establish Nazism within the very tissues of Democracy—a cancer in the body of freemen. They cannot succeed. The conception that the invoking of martial law would put a complete stop to reform is altogether mistaken. And it is a mistake which it is important to understand. Martial law would not prevent the kind of changes which are being made in Puerto Rico. It would merely prevent the violence which is sought to be used in hampering these changes. In earlier months we heard a great deal about the virtues of a regime in which arbitrary rule was substituted for the processes of a liberal government. There was similar talk of this kind in early New Deal days in Washington.

I mention this because there may be an unnecessary fear of martial law among progressive leaders. If we are attacked we shall have to resort to that system. And since we are at war we may be attacked. There is only this one source of confusion that I want to clear up. Puerto Rican reforms will not be lost so long as it is the army of Democracy which protects us.

Not one but many times I have suggested to workers, who felt they had a justified grievance, that since our country was at war there ought not to be a final appeal to the strike. And invariably the response has been just what I hoped it would be. It is well known that in Puerto Rico Selective Service

175

Act has not yet been invoked to choose soldiers for our country: volunteering has made it unnecessary. There are only two of many instances I might cite to prove the patriotic response of Puerto Ricans to war-time needs. These attitutes are well known and appreciated. They indicate to me that the people are as clear about the fundamental issues of the War as they are about the economic issues of the New Deal. The attempts to create disunity, to embroil groups in quarrels with one another, to criticise and disparage the work of any and all officials, have made no impression on the public mind.

That the Puerto Rican people have earned, by their conduct in the economic crisis, and in the crisis of world affairs which finally become War, the right to be called "successful democrats" I am prepared to contend anywhere and every where; and I believe the time is near at hand when recognition of Puerto Rican loyalty and devotion to the ideals of democracy will have a signal reward. I think there is a great thing in store of which I can give you only a hint but that hint should be enough to furnish a clue to my meaning. I can only say that it is a something which Puerto Ricans have always universally desired and which I shall, when it happens, be filled with happiness to have had a part in bringing about. I will not be the one to tell you of it; voices greater than mine in other places will bring the message to you. Other Puerto Ricans have shared in the work for it—one of them is giving you the Spanish version of this address. Just now we are working and hoping.

Meanwhile I can ask you to do no more than you have done: to be patient, faithful, and true; to accept the cruel stringencies of war as conditions which I shall struggle against along with you and try to make as little harmful as is possible. You have my assurance that the War, unless we are overpowered by a force greater than that of a mightily arming America, will not stop the economic and social changes which have undertaken here. Only you, yourselves, exercising the right of free men, can stop them. And that I know you will never do.

History is at work in Puerto Rico as it is always at work in all times and in all places. This is a time for making changes which have been over-long delayed. The occurrances which accompany those changes are bound to take place whether we like it or not. Pay as little attention to the violences of other men as you can. Go about your work peacefully, courageously, and in the faith that you are right. The violence will die down, peace will come again, and we shall discover that what we are now creating has been worth the struggle and is good.

Gasoline and rubber were getting scarce as the war entered its first summer. The Governor had asked for an Emergency Transportation Act which was denied by the Legislature: it gave him too much power. But the breakdown was imminent and he appealed to the Office of Civilian Defense in Washington. Later on they would take control, but meanwhile the situation was critical. Added to this, gasoline shortages began to appear as tankers were sunk. And since Federal rationing had not begun the Insular government had to undertake rationing on a temporary basis. Again he went to the people to explain the seriousness of the situation and to ask their fullest help.

APPEAL FOR SACRIFICE
LA FORTALEZA,
JUNE 30, 1942.

When Mr. Sumner Welles, Under Secretary of State, speaking at the grave of the Unknown Soldier on Memorial Day, said that this was "in very truth a people's war" he meant to be taken literally. The President, as Commander-in-Chief, and all his assistants, civilian and military, live under the rule which is implied by saying that this is a people's war. I include myself in this. But I recognize it not as an idea created by Mr. Welles or by President Roosevelt, but rather a simple statement of fact. There is no way to overcome the immense power of Germany and Japan except as the idea grows in people's minds that the way of life they have established for themselves can only be made secure by their own participation. It is not only a war of military force, but also a war of civilian cooperation

Saying that this a people's war means that there must be participation in the actual carrying on of operations. Selective Service is one evidence of Democracy. It draws on every class and every ability in the community without favor or opportunity for evasion. But there are other evidences. There is the fact, for instance, that a great deal of this war is being fought with a new weapon, the airplane, which has redefined the meaning of "front" and established civilians along with soldiers, women and children along with men, as objects of attack and subjection. That is why Civilian Defense is equally important with military defense and it is why civilians have a legitimate part to play, not only as they go about their ordinary occupations but in matters of war itself.

It is also a technical war, a war of machines, of power, of swift transportation, and civilian participation is not limited, either, to merely making airplanes, tanks, and other weapons of war; but extends in Russia, for instance, to guerrilla operations which are an important method of hurting the enemy. Our part up to now, in the civilian war, is a milder one—the sacrifice of luxuries and conveniences so that power and machines may be mobilized where they will be most effective. That we can do even if we are far from any theatre of operation. And we can do it loyally.

In this general setting, as a part of the people's war, I should like to discuss with you the problems associated with transportation and the use of power. You have been asked already to make some sacrifices. You may be asked to make more. You ought not ever to be asked to make sacrifices which are not necessary to the war effort. On the other hand, I am confident that you will not withhold cooperation in any measure which you understand to be clearly necessary. It has been so in the past and I am sure it will be so in the future.

You understand that all of Puerto Rico's oil and gasoline comes from overseas in tanker ships. You understand that these have been special targets for the submarines which infest the waters around us. The men of the merchant service and especially those who go to sea on tankers have a record of service already which is heroic. It is quite literally true to say in these days and months that gasoline and fuel oil are sailors' blood. We ought not to use them for frivolous purposes.

This is quite apart from the fact that tankers which are saved from coming to Puerto Rico can go to the fighting fronts. But for both reasons we are called upon to do all within our power to economize, to refrain from the use of every unnecessary drop of oil and gasoline. In this respect Puerto Rico has not until just recently done as much as ought to be done, any more than the rest of the country has. Furthermore, it ought to be made clear that the determination of how much sacrifice is necessary in each place is not a matter to be determined in that place. It has to be done by some wider, some over-all authority. In other words, rationing has not and can not be a responsibility of any local government. It has to be the responsibility of the Federal Government.

The problem of building up an organization capable of handling such an immense problem all over the country, however, has made it necessary for local governments to fill in while an organization is being perfected. I am told now that the Federal Government will soon be in a position to undertake rationing of oil and gasoline in Puerto Rico. In the meantime I am asking our local committees, together with the Food and Supplies Commission, to go on doing what they can. I am well aware, however, that they cannot do much unless there is sincere cooperation among consumers.

You know as well as I that certain services must be kept going until the last reserves are gone. Food deliveries must be made from farm to city, busses and públicos must be kept running so that people can reach their work, power must be kept flowing through electric lines, even on a reduced basis, so that operating rooms in hospitals may be lighted, so that Army and Navy searchlights may be kept in operation, trucks and tractors be kept going on which our economic life depends. In order to save our gasoline and oil for such services as these we must not use our automobiles unnecessarily, we must not use electric light whenever we can get along without it, we must learn to walk again whenever walking will do. We must learn again the pleasures of staying at home.

Even so we shall have other emergencies such as that from which we have just emerged. We must not allow our reserves of oil and gasoline to become exhausted. For this, drastic measures are still necessary. Street lights have been turned off early in the night. Gasoline has been withdrawn from all but the most vitally necessary uses. I have no doubt that some of you have a grievance because this may seem to have been done arbitrarily or unfairly. I hope there has been very little feeling of this kind. You must put it down to the fact that the severity of the emergency could not have been anticipated and that measures of control have had to be devised very hastily. We shall improve as time goes on.

There has been a real sharing of sacrifice. Merchants have had to stop their illuminated signs, people have had to make their way through unlighted streets, housewives have had to walk long distances to market and carry their purchases home. Farmers have had trouble getting their produce to town. But you ought to know that during these last weeks the Army, for instance, has also reduced its consumption of gasoline by one-half. I could give you many instances of the same sort of thing. There has, after all, been a rough equality which we shall improve in time.

Transportation is not limited altogether by the lack of gasoline. We shall find that in the long run a far more serious problem will be our inability to renew tires and to buy new vehicles. That is a situation which I have anticipated for many months and have spoken of again and again but which many people, so long as cars and busses run, seemed to be unable to visualize. In anticipation of it I asked the Legislature to pass an emergency transportation law which would allow me to pool cars and trucks, equalize sacrifices, and to use every resource for moving people and goods to the utmost efficiency at all times. To do this I proposed that private automobiles should be publicly used, that trucks should be managed so that they should not carry a load to town and go back empty or vice versa. Those elements in Puerto Rican life who have not been able to understand the reality of the present emergency, and who still hope that business may go on as usual, defeated that law. We are now in more desperate need of it than we then were. I am, I have to tell you, powerless to act.

There was passed, however, a law which established a Transportation Authority. This was not intended particularly to meet the present emergency but rather to be a continuing agency in insular life. It is my belief that as time goes on it will come to be an accepted institution, useful both to those who use transportation services and to those who manage and help to operate them. The new Authority may, itself, if necessary, operate bus lines, or it may, on the other hand, help to organize or participate in the operation of services established by private companies or cooperatives. It is an institution in which I hope you will take pride and whose operation you will watch and guard because it belongs, and always will belong to the people of Puerto Rico.

It ought to be a source of gratification, too, for you that this emergency could not have been met at all, that we might well have been without refrigeration or lighting, if it were not for the service built up through the years by the publicly owned hydroelectric system, the Water Resources Authority. The electric current from the dams and power houses which usually serve only the South side of the Island has for some time been turned into the northern system, thus reducing the consumption of fuel öil.

Indeed the proper management of all power resources has been seen more and more clearly to require interconnection everywhere. If there were rain and the Carite reservoir was full, that ought to be called on; if Garzas had the most water, the power ought to come from there; and only if there were no water available, ought fuel oil to be used.

Considering these benefits from single management and the excellent record of the public system, the Federal Government, as part of the war effort, has now decided to take over the private plants and integrate them with the Water Resources Authority System. This is not only a step in economical power production but a singular vindication of those who have fought so long for public power. Again and again the policy has been laid down by the Legislature. Again and again ways to delay have been found. That is now past. The power resources of this Island—all of them—now belong to the people.

So far in this war, neither the people of Puerto Rico nor their soldiers have had an active part to play at home. Whether the war will come to us I cannot tell you but that we shall go to the war I can tell you very clearly. Our soldiers will go and we may go. We shall be represented in the tankers which we do not use for gasoline, in the food we save to go to the fighting fronts, in the support we give to the American Red Cross, the U.S.O., and other organizations which support the services. You may work in that most important of all civilian jobs, Civilian Defense; but most of all you may have your part in remaining tranquil under provocation; in not believing, ever, those who are still trying to create confusion; you can be patient with improvised regulations; you can help me and other officials as we try to do our best for you and for the cause we represent.

Governor Tugwell had not hesitated to ask the Puerto Rican people to sacrifice for the war effort. When July 4th came he did not hesitate to say that they should share in the freedoms to be won with the peace.

As we look back on such historic occasions as the signing
of the Declaration of Independence, we are apt to over-sim-
plify the issue which triumphed; to overlook the turbulent
incidents which preceded action; and not to remember that
a minority—often a large one—disputed the wisdom of what
was about to be done — sometimes with violence and ill
manners.

It was so, we are now told, with the Declaration. From
my histories in school and college I had a very definite impression of what took place in the afternoon of 4 July 1776:
a group of elderly patriots, having endured an oppressive
absentee administration as long as was humanly possible,
took resolves which were inscribed immediately on enduring
parchment. I assumed that it was done without much debate
in an exalted state of indignation.

Of course it did not happen that way at all. The resolve
to be independent was taken first on 2 July, not 4 July. On
the Second only the form was approved. The New York
delegates were not empowered to sign until 9 July; and the
inscription, in which John Hancock figured so prominently,
was not actually done until 2 August, and then quite without
ceremony. Some of the gentlemen were so conscious of having become subject to hanging for treason that the names of
the actual signers were not published until the following
January.

These are facts which are not very important and they
do not detract from the momentousness of the decision. That
they were not in my school history shows, however, a dangerous adult weakness in dealing with youth. For youths
become men and women, often, with no more knowledge of
such events than was entrusted to them in school. And the
happenings of the past come to seem simple and uncontested,
rather than what they were: bitterly fought issues which
aroused the same passions and led to the same divisions as
those of the present.

The lesson we ought to learn from such struggles among
friends and neighbors as the long one which preceded the
Declaration is that such decisions are almost always taken

in the atmosphere and mood of controversy, recrimination, political manouvering and bitter dissent—similar to those we experience in our time. All was not calm and clear in those Philadelphia summer days. The dignified and determined gentlemen of Philadelphia were quite like ourselves: they were moved by their own reading of events and their view of what the future ought to be. Sometimes their public judgments were influenced by their private interests. Sometimes controversy descended to intrigue.

That out of it all came first the Declaration and then the Constitution ought to comfort us. As we find only confusion in our hearts on public questions; as we feel that accident plays too important a part nowadays in guiding events; as we see small men entrusted with large tasks; it is a relief to know that Hancock was once a candidate for General of the armies in opposition to Washington; or that Robert Morris and John Dickinson disapproved of Independence and that they absented themselves on the day the vote was taken; or that Sam Adams, who pushed and manoeuvered until he had his way, was considered to be, along with Tom Paine, the worst radical experimenter of his time.

The Declaration would have had a better effect for its purpose if it could have been definitely acted on in the Spring when it was first proposed. The opposition to it was so serious on 8 and 10 of June, when the Congress considered it in Committee of the whole, that further debate was postponed to 1 July. It was after this debate that Edward Rutledge of South Carolina wrote to John Jay: "The sensible part of the House opposed the motion; . . . they saw no wisdom in a Declaration of Independence, nor any other purpose to be enforced by it, but placing ourselves in the Power of those with whom we mean to treat, giving our Enemy Notice of our Intentions before we had taken any steps to execute them . . ."

For the issue here was not, in 1776, whether the colonies should be independent. That had been settled long since and the Continental Congress was in being and its army in the field. The question was: what kind of independence? Many patriots still did not contemplate *separation* along with *equality*. The Declaration came out of a quarrel over ways and means of getting foreign support. There were those who felt that France and Spain would assist only if the Colonies cut all connections with Great Britain; and these triumphed on the day we celebrate. Actually, that assistance was not forthcoming nearly as soon as was hoped and might have come in any case. The Declaration probably did not help in what it was intended to do. But it did remove the stigma of dependency, thus giving hope to people everywhere who were governed from afar.

We are justified in celebrating the achievement not because of the false formalisms of literary history, but because out of the deep divisions of the time there arose a classic monument of the spirit. The hesitations and muddlings which surrounded its creation have sunk into insignificance in the long perspective of time. We should be right to forget altogether the surrounding unpleasantness if it did not lead us to so false a view of our own struggles. If it is not indicated that we have advanced since 1776, it helps a good deal to know that men then were actuated by the same, sometimes exalted, sometimes ignoble, motives, that they engaged in the same quarrels—and that only in the minds of a few did there exist a clear perception of what must be done and the means for its doing. It helps also to know that this perception was irresistible and that all opposition failed.

That Declaration did not end colonialism; but it removed that system to a moral category which made it indefensible; and so it determined that some day it would vanish. During the nineteenth century there were actually more subject peoples than at any time in the world's history. But this was because the lesson had not yet penetrated the minds and institutions of men in other nations. The United States of America stood as a reproach to all nations who sought to govern others without their consent. Popular leaders without number have quoted Jefferson. It was written there that some day all men would be free. No delay, no prolonged setback, no apparent victories of Empire, could conceal the elemental meaning of these phrases.

There have been times when, flushed with strength, and impressed with others' seeming successes in exploitation, our own nation has wavered. We have had moments of condescension during which our own superiority has seemed indisputable and the subjection of others only a natural corollary. But there is no man in all the Americas now who does not know that the United States has recovered from her slight attack of 'colonialism. The way out of that sickness was a little difficult. It was found for the Philippines in the granting of complete independence. It was begun for Puerto Rico in granting the present Organic Act; but only begun; there is more to do. The intimate economic relations between this Island and the United States, and the size of the population which has grown to be dependent on them, is the factor which is at once most important, and to many Puerto Ricans' most difficult. They stand in a relationship which is the reverse of that which existed between Britain and her colonies in 1776. The United States does not exploit Puerto Rico. On the contrary, she is helping in the liquidation of absentee control of a large part of the Island's chief industry. In many other ways, too, a clear showing of fraternal friendship has been made.

I do not feel, and I think other citizens of the United States do not feel, that this should determine our ultimate relationship. It is my view that Puerto Rico's future depends on closer rather than looser ties with the United States; but that that decision ought to be made freely by all citizens, not by a few capitalists who prefer no disturbance of their investments.

This moral problem of the United States in Puerto Rico is surely as hard a one as ever confronted a nation. To put Puerto Rico outside the tariff and quota walls of the nation would bring quick ruin. To keep Puerto Rico inside without a clear showing of desire would always stand as a reproach to democratic professions. Sooner or later Puerto Ricans must be allowed to choose and must accept the responsibilities of choosing for themselves.

I speak to you of this problem on Independence Day because some reference to it is so obviously called for in these times. If I do not know a complete answer, that does not excuse avoidance. I believe if we cannot solve all the questions on paper, in advance, we may be able to *work them out,* bit by bit, step by step, thinking and contriving as we go. There are some re-arrangements from which no dissent would be likely. Those might be proposed at once. Others will require discussion, thought and the gathering of consent.

There will be acrimony, perhaps, certainly an impassioned taking of sides. But there is controversy in the making of every great decision. There was recently as we prepared to join the United Nations. There was in 1776, as I have noted, when the Declaration was under discussion. Our present hesitations will be incidents which some day will have been forgot as we have now so generally forgot the controversies of 1776.

As Puerto Rico's great issues are debated in the future the danger is real, it seems to me, that much of the discussion may be irrelevant. The world has changed since 1776 in ways which political leaders often seem not to have grasped. In the sailing-ship, stage-coach world of the eighteenth century, independence for the British colonies was a way of asserting the equal dignity of men. The right to participate in the decisions which affect their fate is an issue now between the democratic and the totalitarian nations. But independence, even for big nations, may not be the way to that end. When we win this war, the most important feature of the Peace will be the atmosphere of *interdependence* in which it will be shaped. All men will at last be equal—not in rights to exploit others to exclude others from the world's resources, or to maintain the old forms of sovereignty, but in rights to peace, to security, and to decency in living.

Men have got to learn that they cannot maintain a world in which equality among the races and among nations is not actually organized. If the attempted return to medievalism is defeated, we must accept the commitment to its alternative. That is Democracy. And we must not only cherish it in our hearts but accept it as the principle on which we shall reconstruct society.

The Governor had urged President Roosevelt to ask Congress for $15,000,000 to encourage the sugar planters to grow food on their idle lands. The President had done so, but Resident Commissioner Pagán had succeeded in persuading a House committee that the money was not needed. The Governor was determined, however, and at his insistence the bill appeared in another form in the Senate. There he made the island's needs abundantly clear at a public hearing in July 1942.

GOVERNOR'S STATEMENT BEFORE THE SUB-COMMITTEE OF THE SENATE APPROPRIATIONS COMMITTEE CONSIDERING THE FIRST SUPPLE-MENTAL NATIONAL DEFENSE APPROPRIATION BILL FOR 1943.

The island of Puerto Rico in normal times imports 36 per cent of its total food supply and a much higher percentage of its basic foods, notably rice, codfish, beans, lard and other pork products.

War, Navy and Shipping Administration officials say that the supplying of widely separated fronts in a global war will make it impossible to ship to Puerto Rico the amounts of food necessary to take care of its requirements.

Humane considerations demand that widespread hunger be averted. Further, it must not be forgot that Puerto Rico is a major base in defense of the Panama Canal, and that military and naval garrisons must also be supplied partly with local produce.

What can be done about it?

There are several things, and all of them are in various stages of development.

First is the working out of a plan of operation and protection of shipping whereby we will get maximum use of the few ships at our disposition.

Second is the establishing of a system of priorities to guarantee that ships which do reach the island will carry only essential commodities.

Third is rationing, to conserve available supplies of food and distribute them as fairly as possible.

Fourth, AND MOST IMPORTANT OF ALL, WHEN ONE FACES THE POSSIBILITY THAT THE ISLAND COULD BE WHOLLY ISOLATED FOR AN INDEFINITE PERIOD, IS EXPANSION OF FOOD PRODUCTION IN PUERTO RICO ITSELF.

More than a year ago, the need for increasing food crops was foreseen and a program initiated. A preliminary survey recently made by the Extension Service of the U. S. Department of Agriculture indicates that this program has raised food crop acreage 30 per cent above the acreage reported by the 1940 census. Unfortunately, this increase is not as im-

197

portant as it might appear. The acreage planted in food crops after the increase amounted to only 425,000 of the Island's 2,000,000 acres. The relative effect of what has been accomplished will be clear if it is recalled that farm experts have said that even if all the land suitable for food crops were planted in food crops, there would not be enough food for Puerto Rico's 2,000,000 people.

Then, too, the burden of the increase up to this time has been carried almost exclusively by independent farmers owning small parcels of land. A much greater production by this group cannot be expected. The small farms generally lack sufficient capital, modern equipment, management and organization. In addition, a very high proportion of the land farmed by this group is of low productivity, and in many cases the holdings are so small that the farmers can grow only enough to feed their own families.

The situation is critical. It demands rapid, mass production. Like all war measures, the food crop program cannot risk the danger of being too little or too late. As has been shown, it is a practical impossibility to grow too much food in Puerto Rico. But even if a surplus were possible, it would be an insignificant price to pay to prevent the undermining of morale which accompanies hunger.

To the extent that suitable land, labor and equipment are available in areas not devoted to sugar cane production, these areas should be used for food planting. But it is clear that the large estates on which sugar is grown have the best land, they have the labor, they have the necessary equipment, and they have the organization and the managing skill.

The same shipping situation which prevents the island from getting enough food also prevents the sugar growers from exporting their total output of sugar. With all available storage space filled to capacity, less than half of the current year crop has been shipped. And for next year the prospects are that an even smaller amount will be moved. These are facts which must be established by the War Production Board and other agencies. But they are substantially correct. Under these circumstances it would be a tragic waste of productive land to plant sugar cane on all of the land planned to be devoted to that purpose.

In this connection, there is another fact which I should like to point out. Puerto Rico has many people and little land, especially little arable land. As a result, practically every arable acre is used for export crops or for food and stock feed. Acreage given to feed crops is relatively small and cannot safely be reduced. The island now must import most of its cattle feed, and dairy herds already are far below a level adequate for even marginal nutrition of the people. Any appreciable expansion in food crop acreage, therefore, must be at the expense of export crop production.

The chief export crops of Puerto Rico are tobacco, coffee and sugar. Tobacco and coffee are grown in the interior, for the most part on hilly land unsuitable for the large fields food crops require. Sugar, on the other hand, virtually monopolizes the flat rich coastal lands. These facts point to only one reasonable conclusion in an emergency which demands the greatest possible food production in the shortest possible time: part of the large coastal estates must be planted to food crops.

Sugar growers have expressed the fear that the food crop program will be used to force permanent curtailment of sugar cane acreage. This is certainly not the purpose. We are interested in one thing and one thing only: a quick increase in food output to avert possible starvation.

In recommending the use of sugar cane land, however, it must be recognized that the return from food crops is much less than the return from sugar. It seems only fair that steps be taken to minimize this loss as much as possible.

One plan is to guarantee minimum prices, as suggested by the Agricultural Marketing Administration before the House Appropriations Sub-committee. This plan would also serve to bring into production whatever small additional acreage independent farmers might be able to plant to food crops.

Another way would be to subsidize growers for the difference between the return normally received from sugar and the return which would be received from food crops.

I do not expect to be responsible for administration of the food crop plan. So I would rather not argue for one plan as against another. I do want to see food growing expanded, and any plan to accomplish this would be satisfactory to me.

An important point that must be considered is that food crop production on the scale now necessary in Puerto Rico requires the establishment of a comprehensive, government-supervised marketing system. The Agricultural Marketing Administration stated before the House Appropriations Subcommittee that it intends to provide such a system.

On the basis of the foregoing facts, I recommend that $15,000,000—the sum estimated by the Agricultural Marketing Administration as necessary to do the job—be appropriated for the use of that agency to stimulate food production in Puerto Rico.

It has been suggested that the sugar planters would not cooperate in a food planting program. I do not believe this. I am confident that when they understand the critical nature of the situation, they will adopt the same patriotic spirit that Puerto Ricans generally have displayed up to now in this war, and will make their contribution to the total effort in defense of the way of life which they, as fellow Americans, share with the people of the United States.

Even in the midst of his war worries it was not possible to stop thinking about the human problems of the island's everyday life. He asked the school-teachers to help solve them.

Governor Tugwell today asked the Supervisors of Puerto Rican Public Schools to support the government in "its grave responsibility" of "planning for the future in a very uncertain world".

"The government by itself cannot do enough" the Governor said in a message read for him at a meeting of the "Círculo de Supervisión y Administración Escolar de Puerto Rico." "It needs and requires the cooperation of the best of its citizens."

"You ladies and gentlemen who have in your hands the direction of our school system and the supervision of thousands of its teachers have an unique opportunity to be of service, in days to come, to your respective communities, to Puerto Rico, even to the world itself.

"In Puerto Rico there is much for us to do. No one of us can be certain of actually what sort of a world we shall be living in when the war is over. We can be certain that it will be a considerably different world from that in which we are now living. We can be certain that in it we shall find new problems and old problems with new aspects. We shall be certain that if we make no attempt to anticipate those problems and their solutions, we shall pay a very high price for our lack of foresight.

"Reconstruction in the past world war is a task which can be accomplished only by the united efforts of men and women of good will in every part of the world. More than ever the problems of our neighbors are our problems; more than ever our problems are the problems of our neighbors. It is unthinkable that men and women who see before them the harsh and cruel results of years of economic, social, political and ethical drifting will face the world of tomorrow in any spirit other than one of respectful determination that the mistakes of the past will not be repeated.

"This does not mean that we, fallible human beings that we are, will not make mistakes in the future as in the past. It does mean that by intelligent planning we can avoid making the same errors in the same proportions, in the future as we have in the past.

"When men and women, whoever they are, and where-ever they may live, have the right and the opportunity to live decently; to feed, to clothe and educate their children; to have adequate medical attention; to participate moderately in the comfort and simple pleasures that our society can and should provide; then, a long step will have been taken in the direction of freeing this world from the frictions and sufferings which contribute so heavily to the promotion of periodical war like explosions.

"You have shown in the selection of a subject for discussion at this assembly that you are soberly and keenly aware of the world of tomorrow. I·urge you to continue your interest in these engrossing problems, and to do all that lies in your power to stimulate the development of interest among your fellow citizens."

Shipping grew worse as the days passed. Food planting became a more and more immediate necessity. The Governor, bitterly opposed by the Farmers Association, an organization of big farmers, appealed to more open minded men of the soil who had broken away from that Association in protest against its narrow partisan attitude.

MESSAGE READ TO THE AGRICULTURAL UNION OF TRUJILLO ALTO, AUGUST 30, 1942.

In an island so predominantly agricultural as is Puerto Rico, the farmer has a very special interest in the solution of the extraordinary problems which have developed, and which will continue to develop, because of the war, and its ever increasing effect on our economy. If you can keep your land in production, and market your crops at fair returns on your investments, then not only are your own problems solved, but, in a large sense, those of the Island. On the other hand, if you can not sell what you produce at fair prices, or if you can not even produce, because of not being able to secure fertilizer, then, not only is there created a bitter personal problem for you, but a problem of unhappy proportions for the Island.

As you all know, the greatest difficulty facing Puerto Rico today is that of adequate transportation, to and from the Continent. To get our sugar, rum, tobacco, needlework, and other products to the United States is a task of magnitude; to get the food for our families, the raw materials for our factories, the fertilizer for our fields, is a task of such magnitude that it demands the sincere cooperation of every responsible citizen in Puerto Rico, and the willing aid of our good friends in Washington.

Every possible effort is now being made in Washington to secure the sure transportation to the Island of the articles which we so badly need. We intend to exhaust every possible method of getting you the fertilizer you require. We are reasonably sure that we shall be able to guarantee you a market for your products, a market that will fairly and justly reward your labors and efforts.

I do not, and would not, conceal from you my belief that in the months to come, Puerto Rico faces a situation so critical that even from the most optimistic view we shall be very fortunate to get through the winter without making very important sacrifices. The spirit of helpfulness which has always distinguished Puerto Rican character — I mean that spirit which leads people to take care of the education of distant relatives, which leads men and women to provide for people who do not have blood ties with them—will enable the Island to make the sacrifices and to overcome the difficulties which it will meet.

It had been said so many times that Governor Tugwell would not receive business men and would not give the Coalition an opportunity to share in the government that the editor of the independent newspaper "El Día" of Ponce, asked the Governor about it. The Governor broke a ten-year rule to give an exclusive interview.

**REPRINTED FROM THE FRONT PAGE OF "EL DIA",
OF PONCE, EDITION OF AUGUST 24, 1942.**

Governor Rexford Guy Tugwell said today (Sunday), in answer to a question from a critic of his administration, that his office at La Fortaleza was open at all times to all civic and political leaders, regardless of party, who wished to consult with him on the problems of Puerto Rico.

All that he asked was that these leaders "be sincerely trying to help Puerto Rico as a whole".

"As Governor, I represent President Roosevelt and the whole people of this island and I do not believe I should engage in partisan political quarrels or the advancement of personal ambitions," the Governor told El Día in an interview granted during a visit to Ponce.

The Executive broke a long standing precedent in giving the interview. He did so because El Día suggested that there might be better understanding of his policy if he would clarify a statement he made at a meeting of the Ponce Lions Club last night (Saturday).

The statement was the Governor's answer to a question put to him by a Ponce sugar grower, Vicente Usera, Jr.

"President Roosevelt has formed a non-partisan administration for the duration of the war," Usera declared in essence. "Would it be possible for you to do the same in Puerto Rico, using the experience and advice of the most capable men regardless of what political party they belonged to?"

"Yes," the Governor replied, "if there was the right attitude".

"Would you care to say anything more on that last part?" Usera asked. The Governor said:

"I don't think it is necessary. I believe everyone knows what I mean."

Mr. William Vivas Valdivieso, publisher of El Día, was among the Governor's hearers. He suggested to the Governor after the meeting that perhaps there were some people who did not know what the Governor meant, and that misunderstanding might be cleared away if the Governor would say something more. Did he have any objection?

"Certainly I do not object," the Governor said. "I would have said something before, except that I thought the people of the island knew what has happened.

"From the beginning of my administration, I have made a constant effort to obtain the advice and cooperation of all the leading citizens of Puerto Rico, in and out of politics.

"I have sent invitations, by telephone and telegraph and letter, to the recognized chiefs of all the political parties on many occasions. Those leaders who choose to call themselves 'the opposition' (I never have called them that) have refused to come to see me, or even to pay me the courtesy of answering my communications. The people of Puerto Rico are so polite and considerate that this attitude on the part of a few men amazed me.

"I have been told, indirectly, that the political leaders of the so-called 'opposition' cannot come to see me because their parties have bound them not to come. If this is true, I am sure it can be remedied easily. I have a great confidence in the Puerto Rican people, and I cannot believe that, if these leaders went back to their parties and explained what the island has at stake in the war and how vital is the cooperation of all groups, any party rules which may now prevent cooperation would be changed.

"From what I have told you, it must be clear to everyone that lack of cooperation has not been the fault of the Governor."

Were the doors of the office of the Governor still open to all political leaders, or had the actions of the past offended him?

"This is no time to be petty," the Governor said. "We are in a war. I will welcome any civic or political leader anytime, the same as I always have".

El Día asked the Governor to clarify his answer to another of the questions Mr. Usera had asked. This question was whether the Governor believed he "should take sides with one political party against another, or should he act as a referee?"

The Governor's response at the Lions meeting was that "analogies are always dangerous, and that is a particularly dangerous one".

"As the Governor of Puerto Rico, I am not taking part in any partisan political fight," the Governor told El Día.

"Up to this time, I have merely approved action taken by the majority of the Legislature, which is the voice of the Puerto Rican people. I have been criticised for this, but I do not see how I could have done otherwise without interfering unjustly in Puerto Rico's task of governing itself according to its own wishes".

In the week after this interview was given, the Office of Defense Transportation in Washington, at Governor Tugwell's request, sent a special commission to San Juan to study Puerto Rico's normally inadequate, now war—weakened transport system.

Fully aware that a major problem of feeding the island in a crisis would be the mere mechanics of marketing, the Governor held a luncheon conference to which he invited insular leaders from all branches of transport enterprise, and the chiefs of all the political parties, to talk things over.

As in the past, the Republican-"Socialist" Coalition leaders refused even to answer the invitation. They were not yet ready to put the war above party politics.

Again in San Juan, to the Lions' Club, the Governor appealed for an end to partisan politics for the duration of the war.

GOVERNOR'S MESSAGE
TO THE LIONS CLUB

Probably the most difficult thing about being Governor of Puerto Rico is the impossibility of doing anything that will be popularly accepted as free of politics. The guests the Governor has to lunch, the places the Governor goes to dinner, are seized upon as indications of political prejudice. The Governor almost never has an opportunity to talk with serious people about the things which need to be discussed— matters social and economic, but not political.

For this reason especially, I am happy to be here with the San Juan Lions, taking part in a gathering of citizens who have a long record of keeping out of party squabbles.

Tonight's is a social gathering, in honor of an esteemed leader of the Lions. This is not an appropriate occasion for a discussion of the many problems confronting Puerto Rico as a result of the war. But I cannot divest myself of the Governorship even here and on such an occasion. I shall say just this serious word:

The war has brought an economic crisis to our island. The next six months will be the most fateful ones in Puerto Rico's history. Our only salvation—short of a quick end to the war, which no one expects—is a united front for action to solve our problems and to urge in Washington the special consideration we must have because Puerto Rican affairs are not like those in the States. If we do not achieve that we shall suffer consequences more serious than I can convey.

Like similar organizations with similar ideals, you Lions will, I am sure, see it as your patriotic duty in the days ahead to take the lead in this non-partisan effort for the community good.

All through the summer there was talk of a special session of the Legislature to enact unemployment relief. The Coalitionists threatened to walk out in order to embarass Mr. Tugwell. The Popular Party retaliated with threats of public demonstration. The Governor, worried over falling rum export taxes which provide half of the insular budget, had the session call ready for publication when rum exports steadily rose again and he postponed action. If enough rum could be shipped, the island could pay its own unemployment relief bill. A war tax burdened United States would not need to be called on to help. But it was not to be. Rum exports again declined. On Labor Day, the two leaders of the legislative majority—Luis Muñoz Marín of the Populars and José Ramírez Santibáñez of the Liberals—agreed to support an insular relief program if Mr. Tugwell got help from Washington for the relief the island could not afford to pay. The Governor went to Washington. In two weeks, he was back in San Juan with an announcement.

PRESS RELEASE
TO MORNING NEWSPAPERS

Governor Tugwell returned from Washington today (Sunday) with a pledge that the Federal government would help Puerto Rico solve its wartime crisis "if Puerto Ricans would do their part."

He thus assured the other half of a war-relief plan he took to the mainland a week ago with the support of the leaders of the two political parties which control a majority of the insular legislature.

Warning that Washington "saw no hope that the shipping shortage may be outlived. It is, indeed, expected to grow worse," the Governor stated:

"This makes it more than ever necessary to hasten our delayed food production program, to relieve unemployment and to secure lower prices for necessities."

He hinted that a special legislative session may be the next step, to enact the Puerto Rican share of the war program promised by Luis Muñoz Marín and José Ramírez Santibáñez, leaders of the popular and liberal parties, just before the Governor left on his mission.

The Federal part of the program, "agreed to in principle while I was in Washington," will include, the Governor said:

1. A shipping priority system based on the island's most vital needs.
2. An integrated method of handling supplies.
3. Enlargement of food crop production.
4. Price control.

Announcements concerning these points will be made, the Governor said, "when details are completed, and when legislative leaders have been consulted concerning Puerto Rico's part in the program."

The Governor's full statement follows:

"New arrangements for priorities, handling of supplies, enlargement of food crop production and the control of prices were agreed to in principle while I was in Washington.

"Announcements covering them will be made when details are completed, and when legislative leaders have been consulted concerning Puerto Rico's part in the program.

"Officials in Washington were aware of the deepening crisis. But they offered no hope that the shipping shortage may be outlived. It is, indeed, expected to grow worse. This makes it more than ever necessary to hasten our delayed food production program, to relieve unemployment and to secure lower prices for necessities.

"Officials in Washington gladly offered to cooperate if Puerto Ricans would do their part. I am confident that they will."

On October 26, the special session for war relief opened. The Governor appeared to make a personal appeal for speedy action. As he walked in, the Coalitionists walked out. Gallery crowds booed the Coalitionists and cheered the Governor, who next day sent his formal message. In this message he reviewed, from a year's perspective, his efforts and his obstructions; he explained the partisan opposition to him, and offered it his friendly cooperation; he refuted accusations of extravagance, and destroyed all basis for the bogey story that he ruled as a tyrant.

MESSAGE TO THE FIFTEENTH LEGISLATURE
THIRD SPECIAL SESSION
OCTOBER 27, 1942.

MEMBERS OF THE LEGISLATURE:

When I addressed the executive message to your honorable bodies last spring, I called attention to a developing state of affairs which has by now taken such definite form that measures can be taken to meet it with assurance of their necessity. I said then that very possibly the most prosperous year Puerto Rico had ever had was behind her; that it was necessary to meet an enemy blockade with extraordinary measures; that in spite of the needs of civil defense and of meeting heavy new burdens being thrown on the executive department, it would be necessary to keep expenditures within certain income; that new taxes ought to be laid; and that later on it would be well for you to meet again to carry out a debt reduction and refinancing plan being prepared by the Treasury.

Nothing has happened since to change these views. And I have to tell you now that though you did much to meet the developing crisis then, there remains still much to be done.

Not enough new taxes were provided to meet with certainty the considerably increased budget which was approved. After its passage by the Legislature, I reduced it considerably by the means provided in the Organic Act and have since made considerable savings through an executive order severely limiting the filling of vacancies throughout the executive establishment. But still more savings may be necessary. Or else revenues must be considerably increased.

Nor were sufficient powers granted the executive to meet contingencies in time of crisis. I am well aware that it is the habit of Puerto Rican legislatures to keep within their possession more of the powers usually delegated to the executive than is true, for instance, in most States of the United States; and I am well enough aware of the reasons for it. But that did not seem to me adequate excuse for refusing to pass, for instance, the emergency transportation bill which was suggested. The lack of such flexible authority as would have been provided in that bill has been felt every day since then. On its failure it was necessary to appeal to the Federal Office of Defense Transportation whose regula-

227

tions, thought not yet available in detail, will undoubtedly be similar to those contemplated in that bill. They will go into operation, however, after we have lost six months. There are other powers needed now which must be delegated to the executive. Otherwise, the oncoming crisis cannot be met in any adequate way.

This extraordinary meeting is called not only to carry out the financial plan which has long been in contemplation, but to consider what the Insular Government itself, by using its own resources and efforts to the utmost, can do for the unemployed and poverty-burdened thousands now growing in number day by day. Only when we are doing all we can for and by ourselves are we in a position to ask as a right that further Federal assistance be given. If these actions are taken quickly and generously here, it will be far easier for those of us who must negotiate with Federal officials to see that the deepening depression is met firmly and courageously.

In the conference which took place during my last hurried visit to Washington in September there was worked out a set of principles on which we might proceed and in which various Federal and Insular agencies might have a part. They represent recognized objectives which we must jointly try to reach. That this program cannot be fully accomplished without cooperation and good will on the part of everyone is true. Its principles however, are so important, and their acceptance has been so generous in Washington, that I do not hesitate to ask your honorable bodies to join in supporting and, in so far as you can, implementing them. I am confident that the Federal officials will do their part in realizing the program.

Stated very simply, that program is as follows:

(1) That Insular purchasing power, including income from sugar, must be sustained.

(2) That minimum normal imports of necessities must be assured.

(3 That local food production projects must be expanded.

(4) That consumers' prices of locally produced and imported necessities must be established at fair levels and must be protected with subsidies where that is required.

(5) That any substantial decrease in private employment must be offset by public employment or relief.

1

I should like to discuss very briefly here each of these points. The most important action, in a quantitative sense, to be taken in sustaining Insular purchasing power, is the purchase by the Federal Government of the sugar crop. For nearly six months I have argued for this action in Washington, pointing out again and again that the Puerto Rican crop is the only one in the Caribbean area which has not been supported in this way by one government or another—American or British. When these negotiations seemed about to succeed, the sugar interests themselves adopted a withdrawing attitude, saying that if the government bought, it would not ship, but if they kept the ownership, their influence with shipping companies would keep the sugar moving and so open the way to the new crop. They overlooked the fact, I felt, that private shipping companies no longer function in the ordinary sense. But this opens a question on which a good deal of the controversy over policy in the last few months has centered.

At the time of the meeting in Jamaica of the supply officers of all British and American territories and possessions, which took place 15–18 May 1942, the delegates were informed officially by notice from the Departments of State, War, Navy and Interior and from such agencies as the War Shipping Administration and War Production Board, that shipping space to Puerto Rico, as well as to other Caribbean areas, was to be reduced to a minimum, and that this minimum would preclude the shipment of sugar in anything like normal quantity. The reasons were evident and open: the submarine blockade and the need for supplying our armed forces overseas. It seemed to me then, and it seems to me now, that it was and is our duty to accept this condition of war and to do our best under the restrictions. I wanted to make sure they were not more restrictive than we could bear, however; and also I argued continuously that alternative purchasing power must be provided if our income was reduced by restricted shipping. I began at once to formulate a program with these premises. I am sorry to say that there has not been a general acceptance of this policy with an honest attempt to work out such modifications as would save our economic life. I still hope for it, though the loss of time has been costly.

I proposed at the Jamaica conference, as a scheme to be adopted by all Caribbean areas, the promotion of a great, integrated food production program, using the best lands available and the best managerial ability. I felt that if this were presented as a patriotic contribution to the war effort, it would be accepted loyally and effectuated at once. Unfortunately, I was unable to secure this acceptance. My suggestion was that farmers and estate owners should be paid substantially as much for raising food as for raising sugar and that guarantees be given that any conversion from sugar to food which took place would not be made a part of future quota calculations. These do not seem to have been sufficient. It was claimed that this policy would ruin the economy of Puerto Rico. The war was ignored and other more light-hearted and optimistic views prevailed. This incredible optimism had more weight than the informed judgment of all the executive agencies. Fifteen million dollars asked for subsidies was rejected by both House and Senate Committees. It has since been considered again but has not been approved.

This disappointment had to be recognized for what it was: the result of misrepresentation of our situation and of interference for the sake of political advantage. But it could not be allowed to halt the work for Puerto Rico's unemployed and hungry people. For unemployment and hunger were by now beginning to be visible even to the most determined skeptic. For the shortage of ships soon caused in turn a shortage of building material and even of material for maintenance of plants, houses, public buildings and the like. This resulted in cutting down not only private but military construction work. Defense operations in the year preceding the adoption of this year's budget equalled income from the island's biggest industry—sugar. Cutting these off, or reducing them substantially, effected by that much one-half of worker's incomes.

The point to be made here is that only by government purchase of the sugar crop can the single greatest source of income be maintained. For many weeks an interdepartmental committee in Washington has been working on the whole sugar problem. I greatly hope that one result of this work will be the purchase of the 1943 crop. And other

Insular products have not been forgot simply because this is the biggest. Other agencies, Federal and Insular, are working to maintain the income from these as well.

2

The second point is that minimum normal imports of necessities must be maintained. It is certainly well enough known, I think, that my own office, the Division of Territories of the Department of the Interior, and the Anglo-American Caribbean Commission, of which I am a member, have made strenuous efforts to assure the supply of necessities for Puerto Rico ever since the crisis began. These efforts have not taken the form desired by those who wanted only to pursue a wholly business-as-usual policy. The restriction on shipping has been loyally accepted, except that the minimum guarantee of the War Shipping Administration was increased at my earnest solicitation, and is not yet sufficient, in my opinion, for our minimum needs—a point on which further representations have been made. This acceptance is necessary, once our minimum requirements are provided for, if we are to do our part in the war. I will freely confess that I am tormented by the agonies of those allies of our nation whose lives are being sacrificed daily for lack of ships to carry the war supplies piled in American ports. And I do not believe that a matter of convenience to anyone, a change in the way of doing business, a reorganization of economic life, ought to weigh, for an instant, in the balance of judgment among those who must decide how ships will be allocated. Only the most pressing needs of our economy should be considered.

We are doing better in one respect, at least. When priorities first began to be examined cargoes coming to Puerto Rico contained as little as 40 percent of what might be called necessities. They now contain about 75 per cent. When the fact became known that precious space was thus wasted, it was sought to have controls applied which would insure that such shipping as could be obtained would be used to best advantage. Such a system is now the responsibility of the Division of Territories which decides what commodities shall make up our incoming cargoes. The War Shipping Administration has a newly established representative here in Puerto Rico who decides on the composition

231

of outgoing cargoes. He does it according to priorities established by the War Production Board. There are unsettled questions here—such as the shipment of rum, so necessary for our revenue structure—but at least an orderly method has been established.

But there were other questions to be decided in this field. There was, for instance, the question of bulk buying and distribution, through existing channels of trade, of the products received, a system which has been in effect for several years in the British colonies of the Caribbean. There was also the further question, in a world given to war, whether enough food would be provided. I sought assurance on the last question from the Agricultural Marketing Administration, an old friend to Puerto Ricans. This organization is the successor to the Surplus Marketing Administration. For a long time it had distributed free to needy Puerto Ricans, in conjunction with the W.P.A., surplus foodstuffs from the States. Its operations were very large. At times nearly half the population of Puerto Rico received assistance in this way. Also it furnished much of the foodstuffs which went into the free school lunches which are so important a feature of Puerto Rican relief.

This organization had taken on new duties. It was purchasing the foodstuffs which were sent on lend-lease to our allies; and it was, for instance, managing with great success the entire purchasing and distribution program for Hawaii. After our first negotiations, an agreement was arrived at by which the Agricultural Marketing Administration would purchase, assemble and ship to Puerto Rico all foodstuffs, both for private and public distribution. There was a natural resistance to this among those merchants who had been used to buying in a free market and selling as they pleased. But their opposition was not sustained when the difficulties and restrictions inherent in a war economy were pointed out. I have to thank publicly the many merchants of Puerto Rico who not only accepted the new arrangements but helped to carry them out.

Since the special session of last fall, there has existed an Insular Food and Supplies organization, first in commission form and then as an Administrator working under the Governor. After long solicitation the duty was given to this organization last summer of assembling merchants' orders and of making distribution, after arrival in Puerto Rico. Until now, it has been felt best to maintain a considerable local organization. It is, however, a heavy expense to the Insular Government and it performs a function in this respect which the Agricultural Marketing Administration is willing to undertake. Recently, I have been party to negotiations for a change in this system, by which Agricultural Marketing Administration would take full responsibility for the procurement and distribution of foodstuffs. I should like to say that this change was made at my own request. The Food and Supplies Administration, in my judgment, has done a successful job under most difficult circumstances. In relieving the Administrator of this task, his energies and organization will be freed for equally important work which cannot be done by existing organizations. And the expense of his operations can be reduced.

The new agreements between the Department of Interior and Agriculture will be of the greatest advantage to our people. The A.M.A. will now not only supply Puerto Rico with foodstuffs to be distributed through the regular channels of trade and for free distribution, but will also, under an entirely new arrangement, purchase local foodstuffs and establish a marketing system for our farmers. It will take responsibility, in this way, for the entire subsistence of our island for the duration of the emergency. This, together with satisfactory progress now being made on a submarine-proof route for supplies, ought to insure against the worst possibilities inherent in the present world situation. It has to be remembered, however, that this island is under blockade, and that the best system thinkable still requires the risky movement of cargoes. That is a matter no civilian organization can control.

As to necessities other than foodstuffs, the local Administration will function as heretofore, assembling orders and transmitting them through the Interior Department's Supply officer to the Division of Territories, where the purchasing, assembling, and loading will be managed. It will be remembered that a fund was appropriated by Congress last January to be used for assistance to Puerto Rico. This was done at my earnest solicitation to the President who immediately responded by asking for the appropriation and entrusted its administration to the Secretary of the Interior.

233

The supplies for private distribuition sent to Puerto Rico will be paid for out of this fund which will be repaid as merchants receive their goods. An officer of the Interior Department, under my general supervision, will represent the interests of the Department here. This supply officer, Mr. J. B. Fahy, is already here and at work.

3

In addition to the necessary imports, it is, however, as I have noted, extremely necessary that local food production projects be supported and expanded. It is to be noted that they have already been expanded by at least 30 per cent. At the regular session of the Legislature, aid to farmers in securing seed and fertilizer was supported with Insular funds. All the agencies of government have helped, both Federal and Insular. The new limits, authorized by the President, for loans to farmers which went into effect several months ago, helped greatly and the loans have been given sympathetic and competent handling. The Farm Security Administration, that ever present friend of rural folk, has also helped by making many thousands of small farmers almost independent of imported foods. The A.A.A., using the full powers available to it, has required, as a condition of conservation payments, actual conversion of land used for other crops to food production. The Extension Service has given advice and assistance everywhere. The Work Projects Administration has made heroic efforts to expand production. All these and other agencies as well have helped in the cause.

We have been seriously handicapped in certain ways. The crisis in transportation, for instance, has aggravated greatly the increase of prices to consumers. Owners of trucks have anticipated an end of their business and have enormously increased their charges. Lacking the transportation law asked of the last Legislature, there has been no effective control of this situation, no pooling of facilities, no real regulation of charges. Our recurrent gasoline shortages have made this situation more difficult. Added to this, retailers have taken advantage of their own opportunities to overcharge. The gap between producer and consumer, always bothersome, has been enlarged.

The rise in consumers' prices, checked once or twice, has on the whole continued, and, aside from its effect on consumers, has tended to shut off the farmers' market. If he cannot sell what he has grown or cannot get a decent price for it, no farmer in his right senses will borrow the funds and expend the labor to produce a crop. For a long time, along with others, I have sought a solution to this problem. The former Commissioner of Agriculture and Commerce, Mr. Isidoro Colón, labored indefatigably with me. We thought we could see the way, but we needed Federal assistance. I am very glad to tell you now that we have found that assistance. One part of the agreement made between the Departments of Interior and Agriculture includes provisions by which the Agricultural Marketing Administration will: (1) establish minimum prices for food grown on the island, (2) establish a market news service, (3) arrange to transport foodstuff from farms to distribution points, and (4) arrange to purchase such foodstuffs as are not purchased by commercial dealers for free distribution.

This, when it becomes effective, ought to go a long way toward a solution of our problem. If, now, our large planters of cane, who possess the best lands and the most efficient management, will assess the war exigency realistically, and, for the time being, confine their plantings to the land needed to produce only the sugar which the Federal agencies advise, and will devote themselves faithfully to food production, we can be assured that the danger of hunger in this island— which I have feared for many months—will be averted. I believe that they will. Most of them, I think, have been willing all along if only they could see a clear way ahead. I do not blame them for a certain unwillingness to jeopardize their cane quotas. I am only sorry that I could not convey to them more convincingly my own information as to the shipping situation and my own knowledge of what that implied for Puerto Rico. I think they have now satisfied themselves that old favors of private shipping lines no longer exist, that private interests are now merged in a vast world struggle in which all privileges are cancelled and in which we must all really work to win. Being satisfied on these points and being no less patriotic than the rest of us, I look forward to their energetic cooperation from now on.

There is one other difficulty: there is no provision in our agreement for any change in retailing; and it is retailers who have taken most advantage of shortages to raise prices

—not all of them, but many. This session of the Legislature, or perhaps a later one, may wish to consider a system of public markets under Insular control. We shall soon see, as regulations of the Office of Price Administration and the Insular Administrator become more effective through court actions, whether that will be necessary. It should be done, of course, only as an emergency measure and as a means of controlling prices. This government has enough work to do now without taking on new duties unless they cannot be avoided.

4

This brings me to the next agreed principle, which is this: that consumers' prices of locally produced and imported necessaries must be protected at a certain level. On the troublesome problem of inflation, I have addressed you before. I need not repeat my warnings of nearly a year ago, or call attention to the fact that predictions made then have since come true. Everyone, I take it, is by now convinced that the rise must be stopped. Aside from the general good effect of increased taxes, which I recommend, we are now to have other weapons. In general, the Office of Price Administration which operates under a Federal law applicable to Puerto Rico, is responsible for rationing, for price fixing and for enforcement. The Insular Administrator has been regarded as merely holding the line until the Office of Price Administration could bring its forces into play. The local organization has been extremely useful in this way. It administered gasoline rationing on an emergency basis for several months and, as we can see now, did it very well, considering the circumstances. There has been a tendency to blame the local Administrator for faults which were inherent in the kind of work his organization was being required to do while it filled in until the Office of Price Administration could get started. We should have been blamed more if we had built up a vast bureaucracy such as would have been adequate for the first months of enforcing new and unfamiliar regulations.

On the whole, our people have been patient with exorbitant prices and with governmental agencies for not having controlled them. There have been many reasons which they cannot have understood very well, such as increases in war-risk insurance and other accessory, allowable costs, the unapplicability of the Federal law to certain kinds of commodities, and the desire to test laws in the courts before proceeding to full-scale enforcement. The period for most of this experimental approach and for the continuous addition of new costs is, I earnestly hope, about over. Enforcement ought weekly to become more certain as penalties for infractions are uniformly applied. And there has been gradual acceptance of the principle of subsidy from public funds to meet costs of an extraordinary kind, traceable largely to the war.

One of the first evidences of the new approach is to be found in the Agricultural Marketing Administration agreement to establish prices for its foostuffs during three-month periods. Working with this as a basis, the price-determining organizations can establish fair margins which can be more easily enforced. Consumers ought to have a better chance for fair prices hereafter. But, as I have said before, the obtaining of compliance must somehow be achieved. If necessary and if retailers do not comply more fully in the future than they have in the past, I shall not hesitate to recommend the establishment of public markets for necessities which will, by competing, ensure that prices are not inflated. In addition it may be necessary to seek further Federal subsidies. This we are committed to do if no other way remains to keep the cost of living within the reach of working people.

5

I come next to the principle that decreases in employment must be offset by increases in public work. This is merely an extension of the policy carried out by the Federal Government, as well as it could, throughout the years since 1933. The situation at this moment in Puerto Rico happens to be difficult because of geographical differences between the mainland area and an island far offshore. As war activity increased on the mainland—"the arsenal of democracy"—need for public employment diminished, and the agencies at work in these fields sharply contracted their operations. But Puerto Rico could not share in war industry. Indeed, as I have pointed out, not enough supplies of various kinds could be secured to keep up ordinary construction and repair operations. To add to these difficulties, the War

237

Production Board applied its limitation orders, designed to conserve vital materials and reduce the amount of useless labor, to Puerto Rico regardless of the difference in situation and felt that it could not do more than consider each project separately. Under the restrictions imposed, and with unemployment growing daily, we have until now been unable to use local materials and labor for an Insular works program which is at all adequate to the need. After months of effort, these restrictions have been lifted only to a limited degree. We have protested against them from the beginning, and must continue to do so until we are given the freedom we need to meet our own severe problems.

Along with others, Puerto Rico suffered reductions in the number of workers employed by W.P.A. This has also been protested from the first. Mr. Paul Edwards, the Administrator here for W.P.A., has repeatedly called attention to our situation. And there has recently been generous modification. It does not meet our needs. But it must be recognized that in administering a policy laid down by Congress, which required drastic cuts in the W.P.A. rolls, officials in Washington have necessarily been limited in their freedom of action. They have done all they could. They have also promised to do more under what seem to me to be reasonable conditions. These include the proposition that we shall do all we can for ourselves. And in this I feel they are entirely justified. You will be asked to provide more taxes and to grant the executive the ability to relieve distress with the funds thus secured. Having strained our own resources to the utmost, and bridged over a difficult transition period, I feel certain we may expect further Federal assistance.

Several weeks ago, feeling the need for a comprenhensive review of the existing situation and a projection of possibilities into the future, I appointed a committee, under the chairmanship of the Acting Commissioner of Labor, to inquire and to make recommendation. This committee labored faithfully and produced a report which I will transmit for your study. It contains a number of proposals, many of which seem to me practicable. I assume that you will find it as valuable as I have.

There is much that can be done to provide useful work which will in no way interfere with the war effort. A program of road construction and repair is well under way. In this matter a great difficulty has been the decrease in the gasoline taxes which are normally devoted to this purpose. I suggest such an increase in these as will provide the funds for keeping our road system at least intact. Suggested designs have also been made for housing which will require almost no imported materials. I see no reason why extensive building of these houses may not assist greatly in absorbing many of the unemployed. There is also much that can be done in conservation of the soil, of water and of forests, and in working toward the park and playground system we hope to create.

There is one suggestion I should like to make, however, concerning the public works to be undertaken at this time and later on in the post war period. These works ought to be largely directed toward enlarging the productive capacity of the people. The torment of Puerto Rico is poverty— poverty in the midst of vast unused possibilities for production. If funds are to be spent, some of these possibilities ought to be opened up. One reason why public works have always concentrated on roads, public buildings, conservation of forest and the like—and I do not mean to be understood as saying that these are undesirable—is that most activities for production and service have been reserved for private enterprise. But private enterprise simply has not expanded sufficiently to increase productivity and enlarge opportunities for employment. It is obvious that it must be supplemented with public work in appropriate productive fields.

Seeing this situation and realizing the emergency nature of the problem, the Legislature created and there has been set up the Puerto Rico Development Company and an accompanying bank, designed to do, in the Insular government, much the same sort of thing that the Reconstruction Finance Corporation does in the Federal government. These institutions are able to encourage enterprises or to start them and so lead the way into new opportunities. There are risks and there will be failures. But even a small number of successes to match the contribution of the cement plant will make any experimental losses worth while. These institutions are the only really hopeful ones for a people crowded on so small a space as this island and having an already seriously eroded soil and a population long divorced from

239

the productive arts. The government, having at last under-taken this responsibility, must follow it up with support and sympathy for those who are working to carry it out. Just as P.R.R.A. began the cement plant in a moment of inspiration, so now a multitude of other choices open up.

There is much said about overpopulation. I have said before and I say again that this is a relative term. For years a downward spiral has been observable—people becoming poorer, their soil eroding, other sources of production failing and these in turn making people poorer than before. The surpluses from sugar production, never so fabulous as they have been represented, have remained sterile or have left the island. The crisis would have reached an impossible climax years ago if it had not been, first, for the relief given under the New Deal and then by vast military works spread over several years. We have come now to the tragic consequence of all the lack of planning, the restrictive management of capital, the exploitation of soil and men which have gone on during the past decades. The damage cannot be repaired quickly, not even, perhaps, in a single generation, since human beings themselves have been damaged. It will be to the everlasting credit of this Legislature, however, that it accepted responsibility and began to act. It must not falter now. It must back up its own creations in action; it must, even at a sacrifice of the prerogatives of politics, assist in enlarging productivity. The expansion into new enterprises and the development of old ones can no longer be neglected. Only along this road can the vast tragedy of Puerto Rican distress be attacked with any hope of success.

It must be insisted that we are now at the beginning of that post war depression which has been so greatly feared everywhere, but for which planning has not anywhere been completed because the war necessarily has demanded first attention. Puerto Rican leaders can be depended on to do whatever they can to further the country's greatest immediate cause—the war. But that does not excuse them from caring for widespread distress among workers and farmers. Allowing people to starve in idleness is no part of the American strategic scheme.

I have found full sympathy and willingness in most places to assist. But we must lead the way ourselves. We must remember, too, that the situation is certain to be much worse

240

before it improves. For this reason, I am sure you will agree that we must pay for our relief and work program out of current income. If we should begin borrowing now we might find ourselves in a desperate plight somewhat later. If we proceed also to put our financial house in order by following out a definite program of debt reduction and re-financing, we shall be better able to meet the difficulties ahead.

Insular Debt and Taxes

On July 1, 1943, the Insular Government will have bonds outstanding in the total sum of $16,363,000. This is not excessive, and it is well within the debt limit. Yet the average interest rate is high—4.372 per cent—and considerable saving is possible by reducing the amount of indebtedness. It is also possible to exchange a number of high interest issues for low interest ones, thus making other savings.

At the same time that the Government owes $16,363,000 on which its pays 4.372 per cent interest, it has on deposit in banks cash balances from the budget and from special (trust) funds amounting to $40,000,000 on which it receives an interest rate of only ⅛ of one per cent. It is not profitable to inquire into the fiscal policies in the past which permitted such a situation to develop; it is desirable now to remedy it as quickly as possible. For this purpose it is necessary to have certain legislation, (1) appropriating part of the existing surplus to acquire certain high-interest issues, (2) authorizing the exchange of old-high-interest bonds for new issues at lower interest rates, (3) authorizing the investment of a certain part of the trust funds in United States, Puerto Rican, or municipal bonds, and (4) the provision of certain taxes to replenish the surplus which will be reduced by this operation. This last is necessary as a guarantee against future uncertainties, as has been pointed out, and to establish funds for work-making projects which will relieve unemployment.

It will be remembered that in my message to the regular session it was suggested that the contrast between taxes in Puerto Rico and the rest of the United States was becoming more conspicuous each year. The new taxes being imposed just now by Act of Congress will make this more evident and criticism on this ground will be harder to meet when further financial assistance is asked from Washington. It should always be remembered that all taxes levied in this Island remain and are spent solely for the benefit of Puerto Ricans. This makes the Legislature's reluctance to meet the United States' standards in this respect even more difficult to explain.

To meet the present situation and to establish a sound basis for the future, a plan is suggested which is briefly described below.

The Plan as to Insular Issues

Part I.

There existed on 1 July an accumulated surplus of $14,653,829.71. It is proposed to spend during the coming fiscal year $6,337,000 of this to acquire issues which are redeemable as follows:

Redemption date	Interest rate	Amount
At any interest payment date_____	4½ percent	$337,000
1 July 1943_____	5 percent	6,000,000
1 July 1944_____	5 percent	1,000,000

After these operations there would be outstanding $9,026,000—a reduction to less than half the debt limit.[1] The purpose of this, I repeat, is to make future borrowings more favorable as to interest rates and other conditions.

Part II.

It is proposed to acquire this remaining $9,026,000 debt by a refinancing operation and to issue in exchange new bonds at current market rates. These would be supported by the same income (or special taxes) provided for the old issues. Authority is also requested for acquiring any part of these issues even if a premium must be paid, provided there is a saving to be made from the operation.

Part III.

The cash balance of trust funds is approximately $20,000,000. Experience has shown that only a part of these funds is used in any one year; the rest remains inactive. Authorization is proposed for:

(1) Investing 70 per cent of the cash balance of trust funds in United States, Puerto Rico, or municipal bonds.

---

[1] There are excluded from this calculation the bonds of the Water Resources Authority.

(2) Borrowing on the security of those bonds, if for any reason the government should find itself short of cash for meeting the obligation of the funds for any short period of time.

(3) Investing these funds in refinancing bonds for the debt of the Government of Puerto Rico or the governments of the municipalities.

MUNICIPAL DEBT

On 1 July 1943 (after an amortization payment of $1,436,276 on that date) the outstanding balance of municipal debt will be $17,004,384. The average rate of interest on this debt is 4.553 percent. Of the issues which make up this total, the following are redeemable within the next two fiscal years:

Redemption date	Interest rate	Amount
At any payment date_____	4.90 percent	$3,530,438
1 July 1943 _____	5.88 percent	134,000
1 July 1944 _____	6.00 percent	9,000
		$3,673,438

This is not so significant a reduction as that to be made on the Insular debt; but the interest rates are higher and the possibilities in refinancing are as great.

THE PLAN AS TO MUNICIPAL ISSUES

It is proposed to make the municipal issues eligible for the investment of trust fund balances. In this connection it is suggested that the Treasurer negotiate with municipal governments for reductions in tax rates which equal the savings made by refinancing. He may also, under the proposal, adjust amortization payments to amounts within the ability of municipal governments to pay. There are now numerous instances in which payments are a heavy burden; and others in which the special taxes levied to meet the issues are insufficient for interest and amortization. With this authorization the Treasurer will be able to correct most of these situations within a short time.

The balance of the municipal debt not redeemable in the near future amounts to $13,330,945. With respect to these issues, it is proposed:

(1) That as many as possible be bought with the surpluses in the trust funds.

(2) To negotiate the exchange of others for refinancing bonds at lower rates of interest, if necessary paying a premium where a saving is to be made.

The General Financial Situation

If $6,337,000 of the accumulated budgetary surplus is used for debt reductions, and one million of other funds are used, a saving of nearly $2,250,000 will result in the long run—that is, if the issues should run to maturity. But the saving even in the first year will amount to $365,165. Also, if $3,673,438 of trust funds are invested in municipal issues, the interest earned will be $1,436,569 as against $36,402 if these funds merely remain in banks as at present. In the first year the saving would be $164,955. Furthermore, if a maximum, say, of $12,000,000—or 70 percent—of special funds are invested at 2 per cent instead of 1/8 of one per cent, which they are earning now, an annual gain of $225,000 will result.

The annual advantage of the outlined bond acquisition and refinancing program which will begin in the fiscal year 1943–44 will be more than $750,000.

The subtraction from the accumulated surplus of the funds necessary to this whole reduction and refinancing operation will result in a usable remaining surplus of $8,316,829.71. This more than balances the special appropriations made in laws effective after 30 June 1942; and these can be considerably reduced for expenditures which cannot be made during the coming year with the prevailing limitations on construction. So that it is necessary only to see whether current income and current expenditure are likely to balance to see whether the fiscal position is essentially sound.

The ordinary budget adopted at the regular session of the Legislature is $20,554,270. On this, administrative savings of at least $500,000 are possible, reducing it to approximately $20,000,000. This, however, is increased some $1,600,000 by self-renewing appropriations (deducting certain postponements which seem to me possible and desirable) and by $350,000 of indefinite appropriations. We shall have to pay out, during the current year, in other words, aside from emergency expenditures, about $22,000,000.

244

To meet this expenditure, with present taxes, we shall have from $22,000,000 up, depending, for instance, on the amount of rum shipped out and the amount of tires, gasoline, etc:, shipped in, and on other similarly uncertain developments. Of course, if the estimate leaves out liquor taxes altogether, and other taxes are considered at a minimum, the amount might be reduced perhaps to 18 millions. This is an extremely conservative figure. The rum tax has yielded more than expected in the current months; and it is hoped that W.P.B. restrictions will not eliminate it for the rest of the year. At this time the total yield seems likely to be more than 18 millions. In fact the first three months of this year yielded almost exactly 25 percent of the 28 millions originally estimated by the Treasurer, rather than of the 23 millions which I have estimated as a conservative guide. To guard against any danger, however, is not unreasonable if the funds can be well used in any case. It is for this pur-purpose that I propose the raising of at least 4 millions in new taxes—just to be certain; and I also ask a certain flexibility in handling current expenditures, and the power, if necessary in an extremity, to reduce the salaries of Insular employees.

I have left out of account here certain old appropriations which have been made by the Legislature at some time in the past but on which expenditures have been made only in part or not at all. The call for expenditures for these items can be variously estimated. But at the present time large construction projects can not be undertaken, for instance; and I do not anticipate that actual withdrawals during 1942-43 will be more than one or two millions. It would be well for the Legislature to re-examine all appropriations of this sort to see whether the need for them has not been met in some other way or has not disappeared altogether. This may be better done, perhaps, at a regular session of the Legislature when there is more time. I shall be glad to submit a proposal of this sort if it is requested. It does not appear to be a sound procedure, however, to carry funds in cash on deposit in banks at ⅛ of one percent interest for years simply because an expenditure is anticipated to be made some time in the future. And to do this at the same time that millions of bonds are outstanding on which rates averaging 4.372 percent are being paid verges on the ridiculous. It would be quite possible for a private banker to use the same deposit of Insular funds on which he pays ⅛ of one percent for the purchase of bonds on which he would receive 4.372 percent.

An instance of a fund which must necessarily be kept at least partly in condition for ready use is the emergency fund. But it is now of such size that all of it need not be kept in cash, after the hurricane season is safely past at any rate, and could well be invested in Insular bonds, thus reducing the amount necessary to be taken from the budgetary surplus for debt reduction.

This fund is a necessary insurance. But others are not. For instance, the balance of $96,862.90 to purchase materials for the women's jail at Manatí cannot be used during the coming year. And the obligation has existed since 1941. The women's jail at Manatí, like the district hospitals, the juvenile home in San Juan, and the minors' annex at the district jail in Ponce—and many others—are desirable projects. But orders of the War Production Board prevent their construction and will continue to do so while the war lasts. The most that can be hoped for in this connection is permission to undertake projects which require no priorities. Certain housing projects might be built that way, but they are provided for now, outside the budget, by an assignment of certain existing taxes. Unless some emergency funds should be assigned for this purpose, no more is needed. Permission was recently refused for building an extension of the Pila Clinic which everyone here felt was clearly war-connected. If that was refused, permission will certainly not be forthcoming for building jails, schools, or other hospitals. I estimate that from $3,000,000 to $4,000,000 is being held in this way for projects likely to remain inactive. This should not continue. Also more recently approved projects which can be carried out, or a refinancing operation which will save considerable sums, ought not to be held up in favor of obligations which exist only on paper.

For some recently approved projects there are larger sums appropriated than will be used during the coming year Probably the Transportation Authority will use only part of its million dollars. The Development Bank will, perhaps, not use its half million before 1 July 1943. The Land Authority is considerably over-financed for the current year. And the sum set aside for Food and Supplies is now partly unnecessary because of new arrangements by which the Federal Government furnishes most of the funds for this work. Both the State Guard and Civilian Defense will use much less than has been provided unless, of course, we are confronted with the kind of crisis for which their functions must be expanded. The $7,487,439 which might possibly be used out of this last Legislature's special appropriations may not actually turn out to be more than 3 or 4 millions of withdrawals. The rest will appear as cash carried into 1943–44.

On the whole, although there are unpredictable factors in both outgo and income, if we consider not book obligations but actual possibilities, we may expect to reach 1 July 1943 with an ordinary surplus even if no formal cancellations are made. And I doubt very much whether at any time during the year even book obligations will exceed resources. The largest uncertainty, after a possible hurricane, is war. Nothing, of course, can really protect against either of the hazards so enormous in their possible size. But otherwise losses in revenue can be partly or mostly made up by administrative reductions if these are energetically pursued and if the executive is given a certain freedom. But I must reiterate that such a reduction is not necessarily to be anticipated, and that it will appear inevitable only if losses on the anticipated rum tax are nearly complete.

At this moment it does not appear necessary to reopen the budget and revise it downward. Unless services of the regular departments are curtailed, the only saving to be made would be by returning salaries to the levels from which they were recently lifted. Unless this is urgently necessary, it would be unjust. All the reasons put forward in March for the increases still exist. And it appears that they can be sustained unless revenue losses are greater than is anticipated. I believe, however, that as an added precaution, the power should be delegated to the executive to reduce the salaries of Insular officials by amounts equal to the increases granted in the last budget. Such authority would be used only as a last resort, but there is no good argument against making it available. Other authority might also be given to reduce certain functions if that appears necessary.

It has frequently been suggested that savings can be made by the abolition of new agencies created by this Legislature:

the Land Authority, the Transportation Authority and others. The Water Resources Authority has even been included in the list on occasion. I am merely being modest when I remind you that neither you nor I invented this organization— Puerto Rico's greatest industrial achievement. I wish that I at least could claim some of Mr. Lucchetti's credit. I do not need to remind Puerto Ricans—although some others apparently do not know—that the Water Resources Authority is not provided for in our budget and that it is somewhat more than self-supporting, and has been for many years past. The same, of course, is expected to be true of the Development Company once its operations are under way, except that, to begin with, a certain assignment of tax funds was made. It has as an asset, moreover, the considerable earned surplus of the cement corporation which continues to be profitable. The Transportation Authority is an operating concern which, once it acquires the properties now in process of transfer, will have operating revenue of its own. The Land Authority is in a different situation. It exists as the result of an Act signed by my predecessor. But that Act was in furtherance not of Puerto Rican policy but of one laid down 40 years ago by the Congress of the United States and never to this day modified. That Puerto Ricans should be criticised for implementing this policy in the only way open to them seems a strange perversion of logic. Everyone knows, I think, that this Act does not embody my ideas of land reform; but if it is what Puerto Ricans want and believe in I shall certainly not take the lead in its destruction. It is a legislative responsibility to choose among the policies to be implemented with taxpayers funds. But I may point out that I have asked the Land Authority for restriction, along with others, of administrative expenses.

The other organization to which reference might be made is the Communications Authority. It will be remembered that at your last session you indicated a purpose to exercise the option which exists by contract to take over the telephone sysem two years hence. If this is to be done some administrative preparation must be made. The Authority seemed the best way. After further study, however, I have determined to recommend, for my part, that the Authority be abolished and that its powers and duties be transferred to the Water Resources Authority. This is purely because of administrative savings to be made. The Water Resources Authority has linesmen and maintenance crews; it has an organization for keeping in touch with consumers; it has, in fact, already a communications system of its own. It would seem practical to make this change at once. If the telephone option is taken up no break in service will occur.

There is resentment also that the Public Service Commission has been enlarged. This comes more from a desire to escape supervision than from a desire for economy. But for what it is worth I note here that the Chairman agreed with me to keep the increases in his budget to half those provided in the authorization. There has been a good deal of loose talk also about the new Planning Board and the Bureau of the Budget. I had supposed the time was past when it was thought more economical and practical to do anything without planning and budgeting. The Auditor confused the issue by comparing the proposed Planning Board here with those set up in the various States, whereas the proper comparison, of course, is with municipalities. For the whole of Puerto Rico was conceived as one unit in the Act. It was not in any sense set up as a mere research group as are those in practically all of the States.

The Planning Act was more carefully prepared, and at less expense to the People of Puerto Rico, than any legislation it possesses. The whole expense was borne by the Federal Government and even now inestimable services are received through the Planning Board from the regional office of the National Resources Planning Board, which was established here at my solicitation. This again, however, I regard as a matter of policy for the Legislature finally to decide. When a functioning planning agency is operating both the legislative and the executive branches lose some of their former prerogatives. This I believe to be for the better, though as an executive the restrictions may at times irk me. And I am certain that the expense of such an agency will be saved a thousand fold by the greater efficiency in government it provides. This is so much a matter of common knowledge, and the whole western world suffers so greatly today from the lack of planning, that the motives of those who suggest its abolition must certainly be examined with care before their advice is taken seriously.

In this whole matter I want to make a final point which your critics and mine prefer to obscure. Increases in the budget for the current fiscal year over the last one are not to be accounted for mostly by the setting up of these agencies. They were financed out of surpluses already accumulated and for the most part they are not in the budget at all. Increases are mostly in other items of expenditure: (1) increases in salary which are far more than justified by living costs and for which no one criticised you when it was done and which should not be again reduced except in extremity; (2) reorganization and enlargement of the Treasury Department which was carried out last year and had to be recognized in the current budget;. (3) provision for the Board of Tax Appeals and the Minimum Wage Board which were established by law in 1941 but appeared for the first time in this year's budget; (4) expansion of the Department of Education to reduce, even if only a little, a disgraceful illiteracy rate; (5) an increased allowance everywhere in the budget for repair and maintenance of government plant which had been neglected for years; (6) increases in food allowances for various institutions to meet increased costs. Put in another way and analysed by departments, and excluding all under $100,000, the increases were as follows: Education, $1,375,000; Health, $859,000; Police, $729,000; Interior, $688,000; Treasury, $509,000; Auditor, $133,000; University of Puerto Rico, $126,000. These increases total $4,222,000, which, as will be seen, accounts for the larger part of the budgetary increase of 1942–43 over 1941–42. I do not believe that anyone will seriously argue that these increases were unjustified or that they ought not to be sustained if it is possible to do so.

Where, in all this, can substantial savings be made by eliminating functions which are not vitally needed? I confess that I do not know. It was a difficult task to cut the budget, when it was in the making, to this amount. Activities and personnel which seemed essential were eliminated; and I was severely criticised, as I remember, for various reductions. It is, as many executives have discovered, one thing to favor economy generally and another thing to accept responsibility for economies in particular. I propose in the present case to avoid great cuts but to make savings here and there wherever it can be done. This, in all, may amount to a good deal.

There are some features of the present world situation which I believe you should be asked to keep in mind. The first of these is the obligation which is on you as legislators—guardians of one of the precious functions of democracy—to remember that in large areas of the world this function has been suppressed. Those who still keep it should treat it as it deserves—as a power to be exercised with restraint and dignity in the sole interest of those you represent—the people. Can you forget in this vast crisis the interests of region, of economic class and of self? Study the war-torn world and ask yourselves whether this is not the time for such a renunciation.

What happens in Puerto Rico can be quite representative. This island is not a large one, perhaps, but it is seen and heard to North and South of us. You may be ambitious—I hope so—to present a picture of legislative effectiveness which will contrast with the charges of futility, partisanship and selfishness which are so much heard. Those of you who have taken pains to find out know that you have an executive who believes in the legislative function and hopes that it will improve. He also feels with his fellow countrymen that the triumph of dictatorship would set back civilization's development for generations. Because, once established, it is hard to dislodge. The institutions of representation grow by long accretion. They are not created overnight. Once they are destroyed they are gone for a long time. But neither are they destroyed overnight. They rather decay and succumb to more vigorous, usually unscrupulous, competition. This decay is internal. Do not let it develop here. And do not permit competition, which would endanger legislative functions, to become unscrupulous.

There are political leaders in Puerto Rico who have not understood the legislative function. Nor do they seem to have understood the special nature of the Puerto Rican executive. As an appointive executive, I have not been partisan. Those leaders who say that I have say it because I had to decline their invitation to exercise my office according to a view of this government with which I could not agree. They contended that I, as Governor, represented them, since they said they were the majority party. They argued this because their candidate for resident commissioner was elected. I do not think that, as Governor, I should act as the representative of any party, majority or minority. I represent the government of the United States and the whole people of the island, and my task as executive is to work with the Legislature in carrying out the people's will. This I have done.

I am honest in stating my view of government. I believe my critics are honest in stating theirs. The difference between us is that my philosophy has worked in practice and theirs could not work because they lacked the power of confirmation of administrative appointees who must keep modern government going.

To paralyze the government would be unthinkable in time of war. I am sure that even my most determined critics will concur in this. So I see no reason why we should not be able to find some common meeting-ground for the sake of our country.

This would give me the advantage of wider counsels than have been available to me . . . . counsels I have in the past invited in vain.

My repeated invitations to certain political leaders have not been refused; they have been ignored. This is not even the attitude of what Mr. Willkie calls "the loyal opposition," assuming, what is not true, that I, as Governor, have had special relations with any party. Surely it will not be continued when these leaders remember that, in refusing collaboration to me they refuse it to that system of government for which the war is being fought. I need not mention that, by provision of the Organic Act, I represent the government of the United States.

I have made no argument against very elaborate attempts which certain persons who choose to oppose me have made to enforce their will by shaking the faith of members of Congress and of friends in various branches of the executive in Washington. This particular feature would be nothing to give concern in ordinary times. But just now Puerto Rico is incapable of saving herself. She must have plenty of help from many sources in Washington. Who among us cares to take the responsibility for the hunger and misery we can expect if this help fails? This is no time to give those in Washington upon whom we must depend a picture of an island grossly divided as it is not; suffering a "reign of terror," which is a strange phrase to describe the extraordinary discipline and loyalty of our people in this crisis; and unworthy of help, because so tolerant of those who are partisan and selfish.

I am still more than ready to receive assistance in all matters which will aid Puerto Rico. So long as I represent the United States here, and have the confidence of the President, I shall favor no party and surrender to no dictation.

I do not regard it as my function to furnish leadership except that which properly comes from one in my position who must help in meeting a crisis of war and in ameliorating the lot of a poverty stricken people. Political leadership here belongs to Puerto Ricans, not to an 'appointed Governor, and there are Puerto Ricans who are capable of furnishing it. I say again that differences are not necessary if leaders will rise to this supreme moment in world history, forgetting self in the vast effort we must now make to save our way of life. No party is big enough to survive opposition to this effort. No party can afford not to join it and help to shape its course.

You will perhaps forgive me if I suggest also that you act quickly on the matters before you. It is common knowledge that I have waited for weeks, even months, while political affairs were being arranged, before calling your honorable bodies into session. Every day of this time I have a terrible consciousness of time running out, of wasted opportunities. Just as we should have taken transportation in hand long ago, we should also long ago have arranged these financial affairs and prepared for the crisis of unemployment which is now gradually deepening. Now that you are ready to meet, it is not too much to ask that you consider first of all financial and relief measures which are before you. If these are 90 day bills—that is to say if more than $\frac{1}{3}$ of you are in opposition—we shall be much farther into the crisis before we can really act. Not a day should be lost in organizing or in discussing generalities. While you discuss, hunger will be closing in on your fellow countrymen. I hope you will remember this every moment of your session. Let it shape your deliberations as it has shaped every action of mine during these past months.

I do not claim credit for having foreseen the difficulties we now face. I am rather disposed to ask forgiveness of the "jíbaros" and industrial workers on this Island for those who have not been willing or able to see that something must be done quickly and thoroughly to meet what we should surely have to face. I knew we should not have the ships we wanted. I told everyone that. I knew we should strain every resource, land, men and management to produce the necessities of life which would be cut off from us. I told everyone that. It was for this that the 15 millions of dollars were wanted. There were those who told me that Puerto Rican estate owners ought to raise food anyway—without the 15 millions. I thought so too. But I was realistic enough to believe that this community service would come much easier if it were well paid.

The food has not yet been grown, not enough at least. As I write this message to your honorable bodies word comes to me, as it does to a Governor who knows many people, from all over this Island, that families who never before were unable to buy rice cannot buy it now. There are lines waiting to buy what little there is. But word comes also of thousands of families who could not buy rice if it was there, or anything else, because they have no work and therefore no income. As legislators you must be equally conscious of these conditions. I beg you not to delay doing what is possible to give relief.

I am disposed to ask your attention for the history of this 15 millions which apparently is not going to be appropriated by Congress. In the first place it must not be confused with the 15 millions appropriated last January and now in actual use as a supply fund. This latter 15 millions was asked by me after the Jamaica supply conference last May. It was recommended by the Bureau of the Budget and by the Army, the Navy, the War Shipping Board, and the Department of Agriculture. It was opposed by interests you know of, with the result that it was refused. Finally, realizing something of the results to be expected, these same interests caused the offering of a new proposal which, although represented as different, was really identical with the first. Hearings were held by the House Committee on October 15. Months had been lost. But also now the allocation was refused, apparently because of misconceptions for our situation fostered throughout the year.

I have to tell you this: we shall have much worse times before we are through this crisis. We are only at its beginning, not at its end. If you are disposed to take this warning a little lightly, I may be forgiven for reminding you that I was right before. We have been without gasoline so that transportation failed us almost altogether. We have now been without some kinds of food, even some kinds which mean most to working people. The time may come when we shall be almost without any at all, unless we grow it ourselves. You have had described to you the arrangements by which the appropriate Federal agencies have engaged themselves to bring us supplies and to maintain a reasonable level of prices. I have participated in these arrangements—they will indeed be carried out under my coordinating supervision—but they may fail. They may fail only in part or they may wholly fail. For we face a ruthless and efficient enemy whose favorite weapon against Puerto Rico would obviously be starvation. Does anyone suppose that our enemies do not know about the vulnerability of our food supply? Of course they do; and they will use it when and if they can. If there is any man who wants to help win this struggle and cannot join the military forces, he can do as much on this island by growing food.

Everything now has been done in a preliminary way to set things straight. We have available loans, we have arrangements for seed and fertilizer, we have an agency which will guarantee to buy, we have transportation experts to insure expeditious passage to consumers. It was not necessary, in any of this, to call on the Legislature for help. These vital aids all come from the Federal Government. If our estate owners and farmers now grow the food, we shall have the problem of seeing to it that workers can buy it. There you can help. Furnish funds for relief. In doing so you will only be enlarging the work of another Federal agency, the W.P.A., whose limitations I have described to you. Furnish funds also for enlargement of the school lunch program and for extending it throughout the seven days of the week. It is pitiful now to hear of the numbers of children who need these lunches and do not have them at all or who do not eat over Sunday because school does not keep. Furnish funds also for growing food. For the W.P.A. and the second unit schools are now growing much of the food these children get and plan to do much more if they are helped.

If it seems to you that we ought to use in these same ways the funds I have recommended to be used for debt reduction and refinancing, I ask you to consider carefully what I have told you of savings to be made and of lower interest rates to be anticipated on future borrowings. For I say again that we are at the beginning, not at the end, of these distresses and we shall need every resource we can contrive—and we shall need it even more than we need it now. That may be hard to conceive for you who are in such close touch with the people; but it is certainly true.

Do not forget to be wise because your hearts are moved. That is the time when wisdom is most needed. By taking these fiscal decisions now, which ought to have been taken long ago, we shall do more for Puerto Ricans, far, than could be done by dividing the dollars among them. It is hardly necessary to stress this point further except to say again that the distance of debt below its legal limit is almost a certain measure of the savings to be made in interest when new borrowings become necessary.

These are days of discouragement and trial. No one can be optimistic except in the long run sense. Puerto Rico must suffer, along with the rest of the world until matters are set straight again. But it is times like these which try men's discipline and their capacity to substitute ingenuity for complaint. You are to do your best as legislators to bring relief: I as Governor will do likewise.

REXFORD G. TUGWELL,
Governor.

LA FORTALEZA, *October 27, 1942.*

In two short weeks, the Legislature demonstrated the Island's sense of responsibility. It provided what it believed would be a substantial contribution to relief. It also provided a refinancing plan such as the Governor had recommended.

After a year of almost constant attack Mr. Tugwell still believed as strongly as ever in the strength and goodness of democracy. He chose another Armistice Day to declare continuance of war against social backwardness.

GOVERNOR'S MESSAGE
ON ARMISTICE DAY, 1942.

Armistice Day is, in a sense, like Christmas. We pause for a few minutes in a year to celebrate an idea which we yearn, deep inside us, to practice every day but which we somehow lack the courage to plan and do.

The generous neighborliness we exhibit on the twenty-fifth of December could make an Armistice universal. And an Armistice, as it was conceived by the world when it was signed, could make us all good neighbors. Yet here we are, on this Armistice Day, hardly daring to speak aloud about peace lest we be thought to give encouragement to a ruthless enemy.

All around us are people asking "why observe Armistice Day in the midst of war?"

There is no reason for not celebrating the Armistice. It represented a great release from fear. It represented hope too. For we felt ourselves wise enough to make it permanent. We were wrong about that. We were not wise enough to make a true peace. We might have imprisoned force for good and all. We might have shaped a world gradually which was built on good will. That we did not do. Force was allowed to escape again to assault an unready people. We can see now what an incredible carelessness that was. Throughout a quarter of a century we dedicated ourselves to our private concerns neglecting to control vast and dangerous economic and social forces, turning our minds away from the ugly manifestations arising in Italy, Germany and Japan. That was not the way to make peace out of victory.

The way to a better world for our children lies in another direction. We must concern ourselves first of all and constantly with the great forces which sweep through our society. We must make sure that force will be in reserve for the maintenance of peace; but not for the enslavement of men. We must keep a vigilant watch for the beginnings of infection and stamp it out with appropriate ruthlessness wherever it appears.

At the end of this war perhaps we shall not make of the armistice a day for celebration. Perhaps we shall reserve that for the day of peace. This armistice seemed permanent in November of 1918; in reality it merely shifted the

261

conflict to other fields, and merely suspended its accompanying armed clash. We shall not deserve another holiday until we have gone through the Armistice to peace.

We should be profoundly grateful, after many years of uncertainty and a final year of urgent preparation, that at last we are really bringing our might to bear in pursuit of final settlement. What we have to suffer yet will be hard to bear; but to be at last well into the struggle we always had to undertake is a great relief. We must now get through it, paying whatever the cost, so that we can come out on the other side where there may be tolerance, mutual respect and justice.

Rarely does a man distill into one short poetic paragraph all the philosophy of a fighting life. Governor Tugwell did in inaugurating the hydro-electric power project at Dos Bocas.

GOVERNOR'S MESSAGE
AT DOS BOCAS DAM,
NOVEMBER 19, 1942.

The sun and the waters of heaven are here made to operate for the people. This is pure gain. Here the energies of men are multiplied; here invisible, untiring servants work for everyone to whom the transmission lines can reach. We begin something here which is a miracle and which may miraculously go on into the far future. It was built with public funds, granted with foresight and wisdom; it will be managed by a public authority. It will produce continuous values. Alongside them its costs will recede until they are hardly visible. No man will profit from it; but all Puerto Ricans will share its services. I dedicate to the use of our people this source of benefits. It was built by them and no one shall ever take it away.